Warning disclaimer The following book is for entertainment and informational purposes only. The information presented is without contract or any type of guarantee assurance. While every caution has been taken to provide accurate and current information, it is solely the reader's responsibility to check all information contained in this article before relying upon it. Neither the author nor publisher can be held accountable for any errors or omissions. Under no circumstances will any legal responsibility or blame be held against the author or publisher for any reparation, damages, or monetary loss due to the information presented, either directly or indirectly. This book is not intended as legal or medical advice. If any such specialized advice is needed, seek a qualified individual for help.

Trademarks are used without permission. Use of the trademark is not authorized by, associated with, or sponsored by the trademark owners. All trademarks and brands used within this book are used with no intent to infringe on the trademark owners and only used for clarifying purposes.

Contents

PHILLY STEAK AND CHEESE SLIDERS

Servings: 12 | Prep: 20m | Cooks: 11m | Total: 31m

NUTRITION FACTS

Calories: 403.5 | Carbohydrates: 45.9g | Protein: 26.2g | Cholesterol: 69.3mg | Sodium: 511.9mg

INGREDIENTS

- 1 pound sirloin steak, cut into 1/8-inch strips
- 1 pinch meat tenderizer
- 1 splash olive oil
- 1 onion, thinly sliced
- 1/2 cup minced bell pepper
- 1 teaspoon Italian seasoning, or to taste
- 1 pinch ground black pepper to taste
- 2 cups canned sliced mushrooms
- 1 (12 count) package Hawaiian-style dinner rolls, sliced in half
- 8 slices provolone cheese

DIRECTIONS

1. Set oven rack about 6 inches from the heat source and preheat the oven's broiler. Mix steak and meat tenderizer together in a bowl.
2. Heat olive oil in a skillet over medium heat. Add onion and bell pepper; cook and stir until slightly softened, about 3 minutes. Stir in steak mixture; cook and stir until flavors combine, about 3 minutes. Mix in Italian seasoning and pepper; add mushrooms. Cook and stir until steak is mostly browned, about 3 minutes.
3. Spoon steak mixture onto lower half of dinner rolls until covered; top with provolone cheese. Place onto a baking sheet.
4. Broil in the preheated oven until cheese is melted, 1 to 3 minutes; remove from broiler. Place dinner roll tops onto melted provolone cheese; broil until tops are toasted, 1 to 2 minutes.

SIRLOIN STEAK WITH MUSHROOMS

Servings: 2 | Prep: 15m | Cooks: 15m | Total: 30m

NUTRITION FACTS

Calories: 568.6 | Carbohydrates: 5.5g | Protein: 32.6g | Cholesterol: 119.3mg | Sodium: 446.6mg

INGREDIENTS

- 1 (12 ounce) sirloin steak
- 1 clove garlic, peeled

- 1 pinch salt and freshly ground black pepper to taste
- 2 tablespoons oil, or as needed
- 1/3cup shiitake mushrooms, stems discarded, caps thickly sliced
- 1/2 shallot, sliced
- 1/3 cup dry white wine
- 1/3cup beef broth
- 1/4 cup butter, cubed
- 2 tablespoons chopped fresh tarragon

DIRECTIONS

1. Season steak with salt and pepper on both sides.
2. Heat a heavy skillet over high heat until a drop of water immediately sizzles and evaporates when flicked onto the skillet's surface. Pour in oil. Add steak and cook until it is beginning to firm and is hot and slightly pink in the center, about 4 minutes per side. An instant-read thermometer inserted into the center should read 140 degrees F (60 degrees C).
3. Remove steak from skillet and set aside. Tent with foil to keep warm. Discard oil remaining in the skillet.
4. Reduce heat to medium-low and cook mushrooms, shallot, and garlic, stirring frequently, until softened, about 5 minutes. Pour in white wine and cook until slightly reduced. Pour in beef broth. Reduce heat to low and stir in butter, 1 cube at a time, stirring well after each addition. Stir in tarragon. Season with salt and pepper. Serve mushroom sauce over the steak.

WILD MUSHROOM SAUCE

Servings: 4 | Prep: 5m | Cooks: 15m | Total: 20m

NUTRITION FACTS

Calories: 388.6 | Carbohydrates: 21.1g | Protein: 4.5g | Cholesterol: 32mg | Sodium: 1923.3mg

INGREDIENTS

- 4 tablespoons butter
- 1/4 cup finely chopped shallots
- 2 ounces portobello mushrooms, sliced
- 2 ounces crimini mushrooms, sliced
- 2 ounces shiitake mushrooms, sliced
- 2 ounces morel mushrooms, sliced
- 2 ounces chanterelle mushrooms, sliced
- 1/2 cup red wine
- 6 fluid ounces beef demi glace
- salt and freshly ground black pepper to taste

DIRECTIONS

1. Melt butter in a saucepan over medium heat. Saute shallots briefly, then stir in all of the mushrooms. Saute until tender and translucent, about 3 minutes. Pour in red wine, and simmer for 3 minutes. Stir in demi glace, and simmer for 6 minutes, or until sauce has thickened.

FRIED TILAPIA WITH OYSTER MUSHROOMS

Servings: 10 | Prep: 15m | Cooks: 15m | Total: 25m

NUTRITION FACTS

Calories: 580.1 | Carbohydrates: 8g | Protein: 50g | Cholesterol: 180.1mg | Sodium: 212.8mg

INGREDIENTS

- 2 tablespoons butter
- 3 cups fresh oyster mushrooms, stemmed and sliced
- 1 cup heavy whipping cream
- 1 pinch salt and freshly ground black pepper to taste
- 4 (8 ounce) fillets tilapia
- 2 tablespoons all-purpose flour
- 2 tablespoons vegetable oil

DIRECTIONS

1. Melt butter in a skillet over medium heat and cook mushroom until browned, about 5 minutes. Add cream, salt, and pepper and simmer until sauce thickens, about 5 minutes.
2. Cut tilapia into large pieces and season with salt and pepper. Dredge in flour.
3. Heat oil in a skillet over medium heat and cook tilapia until cooked through and browned, about 3 minutes on each side. Arrange on a plate and cover with mushroom-cream sauce.

CREAMY MUSHROOM SOUP

Servings: 6 | Prep: 15m | Cooks: 1h20m | Total: 1h35m

NUTRITION FACTS

Calories: 272 | Carbohydrates: 12.2g | Fat: 23.3g | Protein: 6.9g | Cholesterol: 78mg | Sodium: 667mg

INGREDIENTS

- 1/4 cup unsalted butter
- 2 cloves garlic, peeled

- 2 pounds sliced fresh mushrooms
- 1 pinch salt
- 1 yellow onion, diced
- 1 1/2 tablespoons all-purpose flour
- 6 sprigs fresh thyme
- 4 cups chicken broth
- 1 cup water
- 1 cup heavy whipping cream
- 1 pinch salt and freshly ground black pepper to taste
- 1 teaspoon fresh thyme leaves for garnish, or to taste

DIRECTIONS

1. Melt butter in a large soup pot over medium-high heat; cook mushrooms in butter with 1 pinch salt until the mushrooms give off their juices; reduce heat to low. Continue to cook, stirring often, until juices evaporate and the mushrooms are golden brown, about 15 minutes. Set aside a few attractive mushroom slices for garnish later, if desired. Mix onion into mushrooms and cook until onion is soft and translucent, about 5 more minutes.
2. Stir flour into mushroom mixture and cook, stirring often, for 2 minutes to remove raw flour taste. Tie thyme sprigs into a small bundle with kitchen twine and add to mushroom mixture; add garlic cloves. Pour chicken stock and water into mushroom mixture. Bring to a simmer and cook for 1 hour. Remove thyme bundle.
3. Transfer soup to a blender in small batches and puree on high speed until smooth and thick.
4. Return soup to pot and stir in cream. Season with salt and black pepper and serve in bowls, garnished with reserved mushroom slices and a few thyme leaves.

ITALIAN ASPARAGUS AND MUSHROOM FRITTATA

Servings: 4 | Prep: 10m | Cooks: 30m | Total: 40m

NUTRITION FACTS

Calories: 193.7 | Carbohydrates: 6.6g | Protein: 10.9g | Cholesterol: 168.6mg | Sodium: 172mg

INGREDIENTS

- 2 tablespoons extra-virgin olive oil
- 1 clove garlic, peeled
- 1/2 bunch asparagus, trimmed and cut into 1-inch pieces
- 1/3 cup dry white wine
- 4 eaches eggs
- 1/3 cup milk

- 1 (9 ounce) package sliced fresh mushrooms
- 3 tablespoons freshly grated Parmesan cheese, divided
- 1 pinch salt and freshly ground black pepper to taste
- 1 tablespoon chopped fresh parsley

DIRECTIONS

1. Preheat the oven to 350 degrees F (175 degrees C).
2. Heat oil in an oven-safe skillet over medium heat and cook garlic until it starts to sizzle, about 1 minute. Add asparagus and mushrooms and cook until softened, 4 to 5 minutes. Season with salt and pour in white wine. Discard garlic.
3. Mix eggs, milk, 2 tablespoons Parmesan cheese, parsley, salt, and pepper in a bowl. Pour into the skillet over the asparagus and mushrooms.; stir gently. Cook until eggs start to set, about 3 minutes. Sprinkle with remaining 1 tablespoon Parmesan cheese and transfer to the oven.
4. Bake in the preheated oven until frittata has risen and is set, about 20 minutes. Cool slightly before serving.

CHICKEN THIGHS WITH MUSHROOM-LEEK SAUCE

Servings: 8 | Prep: 10m | Cooks: 30m | Total: 40m

NUTRITION FACTS

Calories: 198.2 | Carbohydrates: 7.2g | Protein: 13.8g | Cholesterol: 47.4mg | Sodium: 113mg

INGREDIENTS

- 1 tablespoon extra-virgin olive oil
- 2 teaspoons cornstarch
- 8 boneless, skinless chicken thighs
- 2/3 cup low-fat sour cream
- 4 cups baby bella mushrooms, thinly sliced
- 1 1/2 teaspoons Dijon mustard
- 2 eaches leeks, thinly sliced
- 1 pinch salt to taste
- 2/3 cup dry white wine
- 1 pinch ground black pepper to taste
- 1 1/2 cups reduced-sodium chicken broth

DIRECTIONS

1. Heat oil in a large skillet over medium-high heat. Add chicken; cook until well browned and no longer pink in the center, 4 to 5 minutes per side. Transfer to a plate, cover, and keep warm.

2. Add mushrooms and leeks to the skillet. Cook over medium heat, stirring often, until most of the moisture has evaporated and mushrooms begin to brown, 4 to 6 minutes. Add wine; cook for about 1 minute. Mix broth and cornstarch together in a small bowl; add to the skillet and cook until thickened, 2 to 3 minutes. Stir in sour cream and mustard; cook and stir until combined, about 1 minute. Season sauce with salt and pepper.

3. Nestle chicken thighs into the sauce. Cook until an instant-read thermometer inserted into the thickest part of a thigh reads 165 degrees F (74 degrees C), 8 to 10 minutes more.

EASY CHANTERELLE MUSHROOMS IN CREAM SAUCE

Servings: 4 | Prep: 20m | Cooks: 15m | Total: 35m

NUTRITION FACTS

Calories: 227.2 | Carbohydrates: 14g | Protein: 4.2g | Cholesterol: 56mg | Sodium: 372mg

INGREDIENTS

- 2 tablespoons butter

- 3 eaches shallots, minced

- 3 cups fresh wild chanterelle mushrooms, cleaned and quartered

- 1/2 cup heavy whipping cream

- 1 1/2 teaspoons all-purpose flour

- 1/2 teaspoon cold water, or as needed

- 1/2 teaspoon salt

- 1/2 teaspoon herbes de Provence, or to taste

- fresh ground black pepper, to taste

DIRECTIONS

1. Melt butter in a pan over medium heat and cook shallots until soft and translucent, about 5 minutes. Add chanterelle mushrooms and cook an additional 2 minutes. Add cream and cook until mushrooms are soft, 5 to 10 minutes.

2. Stir flour and water together and add to mushrooms. Bring to a boil. Season with salt, herbes de Provence, and pepper.

SHIITAKE SCALLOPINE

Servings: 8 | Prep: 10m | Cooks: 20m | Total: 30m

NUTRITION FACTS

Calories: 354.2 | Carbohydrates: 51.2g | Protein: 10.4g | Cholesterol: 0mg | Sodium: 562.3mg

INGREDIENTS

- 1 pound angel hair pasta
- 1/4 cup extra virgin olive oil
- 2 cloves garlic, minced
- 2 bulbs shallots, minced
- 1 pound shiitake mushrooms, thinly sliced
- 1/2 teaspoon dried thyme
- 1/2 cup white wine
- 4 (6 ounce) cans marinated artichoke hearts, drained and chopped
- 1/4 cup small capers

DIRECTIONS

1. Bring a large pot of lightly salted water to a boil. Add pasta and cook for 8 to 10 minutes or until al dente; drain.
2. Heat oil in a large heavy skillet over low heat; sweat garlic and shallots until they start to become aromatic. Increase heat to medium and add mushrooms and thyme; saute until mushrooms begin to soften, about 3 minutes. Deglaze pan with wine and simmer 2 minutes. Stir in artichokes and capers and simmer 2 to 3 minutes more.
3. Pour mushroom mixture over pasta and serve.

CHICKEN MARSALA

Servings: 4 | Prep: 10m | Cooks: 20m | Total: 30m

NUTRITION FACTS

Calories: 447.7 | Carbohydrates: 13.3g | Protein: 28.8g | Cholesterol: 99mg | Sodium: 543mg

INGREDIENTS

- 1/4 cup all-purpose flour for coating
- 1/2 teaspoon salt
- 1/4 teaspoon ground black pepper
- 1/2 teaspoon dried oregano
- 4 skinless, boneless chicken breast halves - pounded 1/4 inch thick
- 4 tablespoons butter
- 4 tablespoons olive oil
- 1 cup sliced mushrooms
- 1/2 cup Marsala wine
- 1/4 cup cooking sherry

DIRECTIONS

1. In a shallow dish or bowl, mix together the flour, salt, pepper and oregano. Coat chicken pieces in flour mixture.
2. In a large skillet, melt butter in oil over medium heat. Place chicken in the pan, and lightly brown. Turn over chicken pieces, and add mushrooms. Pour in wine and sherry. Cover skillet; simmer chicken 10 minutes, turning once, until no longer pink and juices run clear.

MOUTH-WATERING STUFFED MUSHROOMS
Servings: 12 | Prep: 25m | Cooks: 20m | Total: 45m

NUTRITION FACTS

Calories: 88 | Carbohydrates: 1.5g | Fat: 8.2g | Protein: 2.7g | Cholesterol: 22mg | Sodium: 82mg

INGREDIENTS

- 12 whole fresh mushrooms
- 1 tablespoon vegetable oil
- 1 tablespoon minced garlic
- 1 (8 ounce) package cream cheese, softened
- 1/4 cup grated Parmesan cheese
- 1/4 teaspoon ground black pepper
- 1/4 teaspoon onion powder
- 1/4 teaspoon ground cayenne pepper

DIRECTIONS

1. Preheat oven to 350 degrees F (175 degrees C). Spray a baking sheet with cooking spray. Clean mushrooms with a damp paper towel. Carefully break off stems. Chop stems extremely fine, discarding tough end of stems.
2. Heat oil in a large skillet over medium heat. Add garlic and chopped mushroom stems to the skillet. Fry until any moisture has disappeared, taking care not to burn garlic. Set aside to cool.
3. When garlic and mushroom mixture is no longer hot, stir in cream cheese, Parmesan cheese, black pepper, onion powder and cayenne pepper. Mixture should be very thick. Using a little spoon, fill each mushroom cap with a generous amount of stuffing. Arrange the mushroom caps on prepared cookie sheet.
4. Bake for 20 minutes in the preheated oven, or until the mushrooms are piping hot and liquid starts to form under caps.

GOURMET MUSHROOM RISOTTO

Servings: 6 | Prep: 20m | Cooks: 30m | Total: 50m

NUTRITION FACTS

Calories: 430.6 | Carbohydrates: 56.6g | Protein: 11.3g | Cholesterol: 29.3mg | Sodium: 1130.8mg

INGREDIENTS

- 6 cups chicken broth, divided
- 3 tablespoons olive oil, divided
- 1 pound portobello mushrooms, thinly sliced
- 1 pound white mushrooms, thinly sliced
- 2 eaches shallots, diced
- 1 1/2 cups Arborio rice
- 1/2 cup dry white wine
- 1/8 teaspoon sea salt to taste
- 1 pinch freshly ground black pepper to taste
- 3 tablespoons finely chopped chives
- 4 tablespoons butter
- 1/3 cup freshly grated Parmesan cheese

DIRECTIONS

1. In a saucepan, warm the broth over low heat.
2. Warm 2 tablespoons olive oil in a large saucepan over medium-high heat. Stir in the mushrooms, and cook until soft, about 3 minutes. Remove mushrooms and their liquid, and set aside.
3. Add 1 tablespoon olive oil to skillet, and stir in the shallots. Cook 1 minute. Add rice, stirring to coat with oil, about 2 minutes. When the rice has taken on a pale, golden color, pour in wine, stirring constantly until the wine is fully absorbed. Add 1/2 cup broth to the rice, and stir until the broth is absorbed. Continue adding broth 1/2 cup at a time, stirring continuously, until the liquid is absorbed and the rice is al dente, about 15 to 20 minutes.
4. Remove from heat, and stir in mushrooms with their liquid, butter, chives, and parmesan. Season with salt and pepper to taste.

CHICKEN BREASTS WITH BALSAMIC VINEGAR AND GARLIC

Servings: 4 | Prep: 5m | Cooks: 25m | Total: 30m

NUTRITION FACTS

Calories: 267.5 | Carbohydrates: 9.9g | Protein: 30.9g | Cholesterol: 77mg | Sodium: 286.3mg

INGREDIENTS

- 4 skinless, boneless chicken breasts
- salt and pepper to taste
- 3/4 pound fresh mushrooms, sliced
- 2 tablespoons all-purpose flour
- 2 tablespoons olive oil
- 6 cloves garlic

- 1/4 cup balsamic vinegar
- 3/4 cup chicken broth
- 1 bay leaf
- 1/4 teaspoon dried thyme
- 1 tablespoon butter

DIRECTIONS

1. Season the chicken with salt and pepper. Rinse the mushrooms and pat dry. Season the flour with salt and pepper and dredge the chicken breasts in the flour mixture. Heat oil in a skillet over medium high heat and saute the chicken until it is nicely browned on one side (about 3 minutes).
2. Add the garlic. Turn the chicken breasts and scatter the mushrooms over them. Continue frying, shaking the skillet and stirring the mushrooms. Cook for about 3 minutes, then add the vinegar, broth, bay leaf and thyme. Cover tightly and simmer over medium low heat for 10 minutes, turning occasionally.
3. Transfer the chicken to a warm serving platter and cover with foil. Set aside. Continue simmering the sauce, uncovered, over medium high heat for about 7 minutes. Swirl in the butter or margarine and discard the bay leaf. Pour this mushroom sauce mixture over the chicken and serve.

AUSSIE CHICKEN

Servings: 4 | Prep: 25m | Cooks: 25m | Total: 1h20m | Additional: 30m

NUTRITION FACTS

Calories: 812.8 | Carbohydrates: 57.1g | Fat: g | Protein: 47.2g | Cholesterol: 152.8mg

Sodium: 1806.8mg

INGREDIENTS

- 4 skinless, boneless chicken breast halves - pounded to 1/2 inch thickness
- 2 teaspoons seasoning salt

- 1/4 cup mayonnaise
- 1 tablespoon dried onion flakes

- 6 slices bacon, cut in half
- 1/2 cup prepared yellow mustard
- 1/2 cup honey
- 1/4 cup light corn syrup
- 1 tablespoon vegetable oil
- 1 cup sliced fresh mushrooms
- 2 cups shredded Colby-Monterey Jack cheese
- 2 tablespoons chopped fresh parsley

DIRECTIONS

1. Rub the chicken breasts with the seasoning salt, cover and refrigerate for 30 minutes.
2. Preheat oven to 350 degrees F (175 degrees C). Place bacon in a large, deep skillet. Cook over medium high heat until crisp. Set aside.
3. In a medium bowl, combine the mustard, honey, corn syrup, mayonnaise and dried onion flakes. Remove half of sauce, cover and refrigerate to serve later.
4. Heat oil in a large skillet over medium heat. Place the breasts in the skillet and saute for 3 to 5 minutes per side, or until browned. Remove from skillet and place the breasts into a 9x13 inch baking dish. Apply the honey mustard sauce to each breast, then layer each breast with mushrooms and bacon. Sprinkle top with shredded cheese.
5. Bake in preheated oven for 15 minutes, or until cheese is melted and chicken juices run clear. Garnish with parsley and serve with the reserved honey mustard sauce.

CAJUN CHICKEN PASTA

Servings: 2 | Prep: 20m | Cooks: 20m | Total: 40m

NUTRITION FACTS

Calories: 934.6 | Carbohydrates: 54g | Protein: 43.7g | Cholesterol: 270.8mg | Sodium: 1189.2mg

INGREDIENTS

- 4 ounces linguine pasta
- 2 skinless, boneless chicken breast halves
- 2 teaspoons Cajun seasoning
- 2 tablespoons butter
- 1 red bell pepper, sliced
- 1 green bell pepper, sliced
- 1 cup heavy cream
- 1/4 teaspoon dried basil
- 1/4 teaspoon lemon pepper
- 1/4 teaspoon salt
- 1/8 teaspoon garlic powder
- 1/8 teaspoon ground black pepper

* 4 fresh mushrooms, sliced
* 1 green onion, chopped
* 1/4 cup grated Parmesan cheese

DIRECTIONS

1. Bring a large pot of lightly salted water to a boil. Add pasta and cook for 8 to 10 minutes or until al dente; drain.
2. Place the chicken and the Cajun seasoning in a plastic bag. Shake to coat. In a large skillet over medium heat, saute the chicken in butter or margarine until almost tender (5 to 7 minutes).
3. Add the red bell pepper, green bell pepper, mushrooms and green onion. Saute and stir for 2 to 3 minutes. Reduce heat.
4. Add the cream, basil, lemon pepper, salt, garlic powder and ground black pepper. Heat through. Add the cooked linguine, toss and heat through. Sprinkle with grated Parmesan cheese and serve.

HUNGARIAN MUSHROOM SOUP

Servings: 6 | Prep: 15m | Cooks: 35m | Total: 50m

NUTRITION FACTS

Calories: 201 | Carbohydrates: 14.8g | Protein: 7.5g | Cholesterol: 32mg | Sodium: 828.7mg

INGREDIENTS

* 4 tablespoons unsalted butter
* 2 cups chopped onions
* 1 pound fresh mushrooms, sliced
* 2 teaspoons dried dill weed
* 1 tablespoon paprika
* 1 tablespoon soy sauce
* 2 cups chicken broth
* 1 cup milk
* 3 tablespoons all-purpose flour
* 1 teaspoon salt
* ground black pepper to taste
* 2 teaspoons lemon juice
* 1/4 cup chopped fresh parsley
* 1/2 cup sour cream

DIRECTIONS

1. Melt the butter in a large pot over medium heat. Saute the onions in the butter for 5 minutes. Add the mushrooms and saute for 5 more minutes. Stir in the dill, paprika, soy sauce and broth. Reduce heat to low, cover, and simmer for 15 minutes.

2. In a separate small bowl, whisk the milk and flour together. Pour this into the soup and stir well to blend. Cover and simmer for 15 more minutes, stirring occasionally.
3. Finally, stir in the salt, ground black pepper, lemon juice, parsley and sour cream. Mix together and allow to heat through over low heat, about 3 to 5 minutes. Do not boil. Serve immediately.

PEPPERED SHRIMP ALFREDO
Servings: 6 | Prep: 30m | Cooks: 20m | Total: 50m

NUTRITION FACTS

Calories: 707 | Carbohydrates: 50.6g | Protein: 28.4g | Cholesterol: 201.5mg | Sodium: 1034.5mg

INGREDIENTS

- 12 ounces penne pasta
- 1/4 cup butter
- 2 tablespoons extra-virgin olive oil
- 1 onion, diced
- 2 cloves garlic, minced
- 1 red bell pepper, diced
- 1/2 pound portobello mushrooms, diced
- 1 pound medium shrimp, peeled and deveined
- 1 (15 ounce) jar Alfredo sauce
- 1/2 cup grated Romano cheese
- 1/2 cup cream
- 1 teaspoon cayenne pepper, or more to taste
- 1 pinch Salt and pepper to taste
- 1/4 cup chopped parsley

DIRECTIONS

1. Bring a large pot of lightly salted water to a boil. Add pasta and cook for 8 to 10 minutes or until al dente; drain.
2. Meanwhile, melt butter together with the olive oil in a saucepan over medium heat. Stir in onion, and cook until softened and translucent, about 2 minutes. Stir in garlic, red pepper, and mushroom; cook over medium-high heat until soft, about 2 minutes more.
3. Stir in the shrimp, and cook until firm and pink, then pour in Alfredo sauce, Romano cheese, and cream; bring to a simmer stirring constantly until thickened, about 5 minutes. Season with cayenne, salt, and pepper to taste. Stir drained pasta into the sauce, and serve sprinkled with chopped parsley.

SLOW COOKER STUFFING

Servings: 16 | Prep: 25m | Cooks: 8h55m | Total: 9h20m

NUTRITION FACTS

Calories: 196.8 | Carbohydrates: 16.6g | Protein: 3.9g | Cholesterol: 53.8mg | Sodium: 501.7mg

INGREDIENTS

- 1 cup butter or margarine
- 2 cups chopped onion
- 2 cups chopped celery
- 1/4 cup chopped fresh parsley
- 12 ounces sliced mushrooms
- 12 cups dry bread cubes
- 1 teaspoon poultry seasoning
- 1 1/2 teaspoons dried sage
- 1 teaspoon dried thyme
- 1/2 teaspoon dried marjoram
- 1 1/2 teaspoons salt
- 1/2 teaspoon ground black pepper
- 4 1/2 cups chicken broth, or as needed
- 2 eggs, beaten

DIRECTIONS

1. Melt butter or margarine in a skillet over medium heat. Cook onion, celery, mushroom, and parsley in butter, stirring frequently.
2. Spoon cooked vegetables over bread cubes in a very large mixing bowl. Season with poultry seasoning, sage, thyme, marjoram, and salt and pepper. Pour in enough broth to moisten, and mix in eggs. Transfer mixture to slow cooker, and cover.
3. Cook on High for 45 minutes, then reduce heat to Low, and cook for 4 to 8 hours.

MUSHROOM PORK CHOPS

Servings: 4 | Prep: 10m | Cooks: 30m | Total: 40m

NUTRITION FACTS

Calories: 209.7 | Carbohydrates: 9.6g | Protein: 23.6g | Cholesterol: 64.9mg | Sodium: 924.3mg

INGREDIENTS

- 4 pork chops
- 1/2 teaspoon salt and pepper to taste
- 1 onion, chopped
- 1/2 pound fresh mushrooms, sliced

- 1 pinch garlic salt, or to taste
- 1 (10.75 ounce) can condensed cream of mushroom soup

DIRECTIONS

1. Season pork chops with salt, pepper, and garlic salt to taste.
2. In a large skillet, brown the chops over medium-high heat. Add the onion and mushrooms, and saute for one minute. Pour cream of mushroom soup over chops. Cover skillet, and reduce temperature to medium-low. Simmer 20 to 30 minutes, or until chops are cooked through.

CHICKEN WITH MUSHROOMS

Servings: 4 | Prep: 15m | Cooks: 30m | Total: 45m

NUTRITION FACTS

Calories: 454.3 | Carbohydrates: 23.8g | Protein: 44.1g | Cholesterol: 203.9mg | Sodium: 1107.9mg

INGREDIENTS

- 3 cups sliced mushrooms
- 4 skinless, boneless chicken breast halves
- 2 eggs, beaten
- 1 cup seasoned bread crumbs
- 2 tablespoons butter
- 6 ounces mozzarella cheese, sliced
- 3/4 cup chicken broth

DIRECTIONS

1. Preheat oven to 350 degrees F (175 degrees C).
2. Place half of the mushrooms in a 9x13 inch pan. Dip chicken into beaten eggs, then roll in bread crumbs.
3. In skillet, melt butter over medium heat. Brown both sides of chicken in skillet. Place chicken on top of mushrooms, arrange remaining mushrooms on chicken, and top with mozzarella cheese. Add chicken broth to pan.
4. Bake in preheated oven for 30 to 35 minutes, or until chicken is no longer pink and juices run clear.

TUNA NOODLE CASSEROLE FROM SCRATCH

Servings: 6 | Prep: 30m | Cooks: 45m | Total: 1h15m

NUTRITION FACTS

Calories: 545.6 | Carbohydrates: 39.9g | Protein: 27.2g | Cholesterol: 121.1mg | Sodium: 785.9mg

INGREDIENTS

- 1/2 cup butter, divided
- 1 (8 ounce) package uncooked medium egg noodles
- 1/2 medium onion, finely chopped
- 1 stalk celery, finely chopped
- 1 clove garlic, minced
- 8 ounces button mushrooms, sliced
- 1/4 cup all-purpose flour
- 2 cups milk
- 1 teaspoon salt and pepper to taste
- 2 (5 ounce) cans tuna, drained and flaked
- 1 cup frozen peas, thawed
- 3 tablespoons bread crumbs
- 2 tablespoons butter, melted
- 1 cup shredded Cheddar cheese

DIRECTIONS

1. Preheat oven to 375 degrees F (190 degrees C). Butter a medium baking dish with 1 tablespoon butter.
2. Bring a large pot of lightly salted water to a boil. Add egg noodles, cook for 8 to 10 minutes, until al dente, and drain.
3. Melt 1 tablespoon butter in a skillet over medium-low heat. Stir in the onion, celery, and garlic, and cook 5 minutes, until tender. Increase heat to medium-high, and mix in mushrooms. Continue to cook and stir 5 minutes, or until most of the liquid has evaporated.
4. Melt 4 tablespoons butter in a medium saucepan, and whisk in flour until smooth. Gradually whisk in milk, and continue cooking 5 minutes, until sauce is smooth and slightly thickened. Season with salt and pepper. Stir in tuna, peas, mushroom mixture, and cooked noodles. Transfer to the baking dish. Melt remaining 2 tablespoons butter in a small bowl, mix with bread crumbs, and sprinkle over the casserole. Top with cheese.
5. Bake 25 minutes in the preheated oven, or until bubbly and lightly browned.

THE BEST THAI COCONUT SOUP

Servings: 8 | Prep: 35m | Cooks: 30m | Total: 1h5m

NUTRITION FACTS

Calories: 367.6 | Carbohydrates: 8.9g | Protein: 13.2g | Cholesterol: 86.3mg | Sodium: 579.4mg

INGREDIENTS

- 1 tablespoon vegetable oil
- 2 tablespoons grated fresh ginger
- 1 stalk lemon grass, minced
- 2 teaspoons red curry paste
- 4 cups chicken broth
- 3 tablespoons fish sauce
- 1 tablespoon light brown sugar
- 3 (13.5 ounce) cans coconut milk
- 1/2 pound fresh shiitake mushrooms, sliced
- 1 pound medium shrimp - peeled and deveined
- 2 tablespoons fresh lime juice
- 1 pinch salt to taste
- 1/4 cup chopped fresh cilantro

DIRECTIONS

1. Heat the oil in a large pot over medium heat. Cook and stir the ginger, lemongrass, and curry paste in the heated oil for 1 minute. Slowly pour the chicken broth over the mixture, stirring continually. Stir in the fish sauce and brown sugar; simmer for 15 minutes. Stir in the coconut milk and mushrooms; cook and stir until the mushrooms are soft, about 5 minutes. Add the shrimp; cook until no longer translucent about 5 minutes. Stir in the lime juice; season with salt; garnish with cilantro.

SUKI'S SPINACH AND FETA PASTA

Servings: 4 | Prep: 25m | Cooks: 15m | Total: 40m

NUTRITION FACTS

Calories: 451 | Carbohydrates: 51.8g | Fat: 20.6g | Protein: 17.8g | Cholesterol: 50mg | Sodium: 656mg

INGREDIENTS

- 1 (8 ounce) package penne pasta
- 2 tablespoons olive oil
- 1 cup sliced fresh mushrooms
- 2 cups spinach leaves, packed

- 1/2 cup chopped onion
- 1 clove garlic, minced
- 3 cups chopped tomatoes
- salt and pepper to taste
- 1 pinch red pepper flakes
- 8 ounces feta cheese, crumbled

DIRECTIONS

1. Bring a large pot of lightly salted water to a boil. Cook pasta in boiling water until al dente; drain.
2. Meanwhile, heat olive oil in a large skillet over medium-high heat; add onion and garlic, and cook until golden brown. Mix in tomatoes, mushrooms, and spinach. Season with salt, pepper, and red pepper flakes. Cook 2 minutes more, until tomatoes are heated through and spinach is wilted. Reduce heat to medium, stir in pasta and feta cheese, and cook until heated through.

CREAM OF MUSHROOM SOUP

Servings: 6 | Prep: 20m | Cooks: 30m | Total: 50m

NUTRITION FACTS

Calories: 148 | Carbohydrates: 8.6g | Protein: 4.8g | Cholesterol: 30.2mg | Sodium: 363.7mg

INGREDIENTS

- 5 cups sliced fresh mushrooms
- 1 1/2 cups chicken broth
- 1/2 cup chopped onion
- 1/8 teaspoon dried thyme
- 3 tablespoons butter
- 3 tablespoons all-purpose flour
- 1/4 teaspoon salt
- 1/4 teaspoon ground black pepper
- 1 cup half-and-half
- 1 tablespoon sherry

DIRECTIONS

1. In a large heavy saucepan, cook mushrooms in the broth with onion and thyme until tender, about 10 to 15 minutes.
2. In blender or food processor, puree the mixture , leaving some chunks of vegetable in it. Set aside.
3. In the saucepan, melt the butter, whisk in the flour until smooth. Add the salt, pepper, half and half and vegetable puree. Stirring constantly, bring soup to a boil and cook until thickened. Adjust seasonings to taste, and add sherry.

RUSSIAN MUSHROOM AND POTATO SOUP

Servings: 12 | Prep: 20m | Cooks: 40m | Total: 1h

NUTRITION FACTS

Calories: 166.7 | Carbohydrates: 21.2g | Protein: 4.5g | Cholesterol: 22.7mg | Sodium: 928.1mg

INGREDIENTS

- 5 tablespoons butter, divided
- 2 leeks, chopped
- 2 large carrots, sliced
- 6 cups chicken broth
- 2 teaspoons dried dill weed
- 2 teaspoons salt
- 1/8 teaspoon ground black pepper
- 1 bay leaf
- 2 pounds potatoes, peeled and diced
- 1 pound fresh mushrooms, sliced
- 1 cup half-and-half
- 1/4 cup all-purpose flour
- 1 sprig fresh dill weed, for garnish

DIRECTIONS

1. Melt 3 tablespoons butter in a large saucepan over medium heat. Mix in leeks and carrots, and cook 5 minutes. Pour in broth. Season with dill, salt, pepper, and bay leaf. Mix in potatoes, cover, and cook 20 minutes, or until potatoes are tender but firm. Remove and discard the bay leaf.
2. Melt the remaining butter in a skillet over medium heat, and saute the mushrooms 5 minutes, until lightly browned. Stir into the soup.
3. In a small bowl, mix the half-and-half and flour until smooth. Stir into the soup to thicken. Garnish each bowl of soup with fresh dill to serve.

RATATOUILLE

Servings: 4 | Prep: 15m | Cooks: 45m | Total: 1h

NUTRITION FACTS

Calories: 251.4 | Carbohydrates: 24.3g | Protein: 12.7g | Cholesterol: 17.6mg | Sodium: 327.4mg

INGREDIENTS

- 2 tablespoons olive oil
- 2 zucchini, sliced

- 3 cloves garlic, minced
- 2 teaspoons dried parsley
- 1 eggplant, cut into 1/2 inch cubes
- salt to taste
- 1 cup grated Parmesan cheese
- 1 large onion, sliced into rings
- 2 cups sliced fresh mushrooms
- 1 green bell pepper, sliced
- 2 large tomatoes, chopped

DIRECTIONS

1. Preheat oven to 350 degrees F (175 degrees C). Coat bottom and sides of a 1 1/2 quart casserole dish with 1 tablespoon olive oil.
2. Heat remaining 1 tablespoon olive oil in a medium skillet over medium heat. Cook and stir garlic until lightly browned. Mix in parsley and eggplant. Cook and stir until eggplant is soft, about 10 minutes. Season with salt to taste.
3. Spread eggplant mixture evenly across bottom of prepared casserole dish. Sprinkle with a few tablespoons of Parmesan cheese. Spread zucchini in an even layer over top. Lightly salt and sprinkle with a little more cheese. Continue layering in this fashion, with onion, mushrooms, bell pepper, and tomatoes, covering each layer with a sprinkling of salt and cheese.
4. Bake in preheated oven for 45 minutes.

SHRIMP AND MUSHROOM LINGUINI WITH CREAMY CHEESE HERB SAUCE

Servings: 4 | Prep: 15m | Cooks: 15m | Total: 30m

NUTRITION FACTS

Calories: 601.4 | Carbohydrates: 44g | Protein: 23.2g | Cholesterol: 210.3mg | Sodium: 402.7mg

INGREDIENTS

- 1 (8 ounce) package linguini pasta
- 2 tablespoons butter
- 1/2 pound fresh mushrooms, sliced
- 1/2 cup butter
- 2 cloves garlic, minced
- 1 (3 ounce) package cream cheese
- 2 tablespoons chopped fresh parsley
- 3/4 teaspoon dried basil
- 2/3 cup boiling water
- 1/2 pound cooked shrimp

DIRECTIONS

1. Bring a large pot of lightly salted water to a boil. Add linguini and cook until tender, about 7 minutes. Drain.
2. Meanwhile, heat 2 tablespoons butter in a large skillet over medium-high heat. Add mushrooms; cook and stir until tender. Transfer to a plate.
3. In the same pan, melt 1/2 cup butter with the minced garlic. Stir in the cream cheese, breaking it up with a spoon as it melts. Stir in the parsley and basil. Simmer for 5 minutes. Mix in boiling water until sauce is smooth. Stir in cooked shrimp and mushrooms; heat sauce through.
4. Toss linguini with shrimp sauce and serve.

SALISBURY STEAK WITH MUSHROOMS

Servings: 64| Prep: 15m | Cooks: 25m | Total: 40m

NUTRITION FACTS

Calories: 322.5 | Carbohydrates: 17.2g | Protein: 26.6g | Cholesterol: 115.3mg | Sodium: 1128.9mg

INGREDIENTS

- 1 pound lean ground beef
- 1/3 cup dry bread crumbs
- 1/4 cup chopped onions
- 1 egg, beaten
- 1 teaspoon salt
- 1/4 teaspoon ground black pepper
- 2 cups beef broth
- 1 large onion, thinly sliced
- 1 cup sliced mushrooms
- 3 tablespoons cornstarch
- 3 tablespoons water

DIRECTIONS

1. Combine ground beef, bread crumbs, chopped onion, egg, salt, and black pepper in a bowl until evenly mixed. Shape beef mixture into 4 patties, about 3/4 inch thick.
2. Fry patties in a large skillet over medium heat until browned on both sides, about 10 minutes. Add beef broth, onion, and mushrooms; bring to a boil. Reduce heat to low, cover, and simmer until patties are no longer pink in the center, about 10 minutes more. Transfer patties to a platter and keep warm.
3. Bring onion mixture to a boil. Mix cornstarch and water in a small bowl; stir into onion mixture. Cook and stir until onion gravy is thickened, about 1 minute. Pour over patties to serve.

GREEK PASTA SALAD

Servings: 4 | Prep: 15m | Cooks: 10m | Total: 2h25m | Additional: 2h

NUTRITION FACTS

Calories: 745.6 | Carbohydrates: 40.4g | Protein: 22.1g | Cholesterol: 69.7mg | Sodium: 1278.7mg

INGREDIENTS

- 1/2 cup olive oil
- 1/2 cup red wine vinegar
- 1 1/2 teaspoons garlic powder
- 1 ½ teaspoons dried basil
- 1 1/2 teaspoons dried oregano
- 3/4 teaspoon ground black pepper
- 3/4 teaspoon white sugar
- 2 1/2 cups cooked elbow macaroni
- 3 cups fresh sliced mushrooms
- 15 eaches cherry tomatoes, halved
- 1 cup sliced red bell peppers
- 3/4 cup crumbled feta cheese
- 1/2 cup chopped green onions
- 1 (4 ounce) can whole black olives
- 3/4 cup sliced pepperoni sausage, cut into strips

DIRECTIONS

1. In a large bowl, whisk together olive oil, vinegar, garlic powder, basil, oregano, black pepper, and sugar. Add cooked pasta, mushrooms, tomatoes, red peppers, feta cheese, green onions, olives, and pepperoni. Toss until evenly coated. Cover, and chill 2 hours or overnight.

HEARTY VEGETABLE LASAGNA

Servings: 12 | Prep: 25m | Cooks: 1h | Total: 1h40m | Additional: 15m

NUTRITION FACTS

Calories: 462.5 | Carbohydrates: 49.6g | Protein: 23.2g | Cholesterol: 76.9mg | Sodium: 743.2mg

INGREDIENTS

- 1 (16 ounce) package lasagna noodles
- 1 pound fresh mushrooms, sliced
- 2 (26 ounce) jars pasta sauce
- 1 teaspoon dried basil

- 3/4 cup chopped green bell pepper
- 3/4 cup chopped onion
- 3 cloves garlic, minced
- 2 tablespoons vegetable oil
- 1 (15 ounce) container part-skim ricotta cheese
- 4 cups shredded mozzarella cheese
- 2 eggs
- 1/2 cup grated Parmesan cheese

DIRECTIONS

1. Cook the lasagna noodles in a large pot of boiling water for 10 minutes, or until al dente. Rinse with cold water, and drain.
2. In a large saucepan, cook and stir mushrooms, green peppers, onion, and garlic in oil. Stir in pasta sauce and basil; bring to a boil. Reduce heat, and simmer 15 minutes.
3. Mix together ricotta, 2 cups mozzarella cheese, and eggs.
4. Preheat oven to 350 degrees F (175 degrees C). Spread 1 cup tomato sauce into the bottom of a greased 9x13 inch baking dish. Layer 1/2 each, lasagna noodles, ricotta mix, sauce, and Parmesan cheese. Repeat layering, and top with remaining 2 cups mozzarella cheese.
5. Bake, uncovered, for 40 minutes. Let stand 15 minutes before serving.

MELT-IN-YOUR-MOUTH MEAT LOAF

Servings: 6 | Prep: 15m | Cooks: 5h15m | Total: 5h40m | Additional: 10m

NUTRITION FACTS

Calories: 328 | Carbohydrates: 18.4g | Fat: 16.9g | Protein: 24.7g | Cholesterol: 136mg | Sodium: 841mg

INGREDIENTS

- 2 eggs
- 3/4 cup milk
- 2/3 cup seasoned bread crumbs
- 2 teaspoons dried minced onion
- 1 teaspoon salt
- 1/2 teaspoon rubbed sage
- 1/2 cup sliced fresh mushrooms
- 1 1/2 pounds ground beef
- 1/4 cup ketchup
- 2 tablespoons brown sugar
- 1 teaspoon ground mustard
- 1/2 teaspoon Worcestershire sauce

DIRECTIONS

1. Combine eggs, milk, bread crumbs, onion, salt, sage, and mushrooms in a large bowl. Crumble ground beef over mixture and stir well to combine. Shape into a round loaf; place in a 5-quart slow cooker. Cover and cook on Low until a meat thermometer reads 160 degrees F (71 degrees C), 5 to 6 hours.
2. Whisk ketchup, brown sugar, mustard, and Worcestershire sauce in a small bowl; spoon sauce over meat loaf. Return to slow cooker and cook on Low until heated through, about 15 minutes. Let stand 10 minutes before cutting.

PORTOBELLO MUSHROOM BURGERS

Servings: 4 | Prep: 15m | Cooks: 20m | Total: 35m

NUTRITION FACTS

Calories: 203.2 | Carbohydrates: 9.8g | Protein: 10.3g | Cholesterol: 19.6mg | Sodium: 259.5mg

INGREDIENTS

- 4 portobello mushroom caps
- 1/4 cup balsamic vinegar
- 2 tablespoons olive oil
- 1 teaspoon dried basil
- 1 teaspoon dried oregano
- 1 tablespoon minced garlic
- 1 pinch salt and pepper to taste
- 4 (1 ounce) slices provolone cheese

DIRECTIONS

1. Place the mushroom caps, smooth side up, in a shallow dish. In a small bowl, whisk together vinegar, oil, basil, oregano, garlic, salt, and pepper. Pour over the mushrooms. Let stand at room temperature for 15 minutes or so, turning twice.
2. Preheat grill for medium-high heat.
3. Brush grate with oil. Place mushrooms on the grill, reserving marinade for basting. Grill for 5 to 8 minutes on each side, or until tender. Brush with marinade frequently. Top with cheese during the last 2 minutes of grilling.

MUSHROOMS WITH A SOY SAUCE GLAZE

Servings: 2 | Prep: 5m | Cooks: 10m | Total: 15m

NUTRITION FACTS

Calories: 135 | Carbohydrates: 5.4g | Protein: 4.2g | Cholesterol: 30.5mg | Sodium: 386.9mg

INGREDIENTS

- 2 tablespoons butter

- 1 (8 ounce) package sliced white mushrooms

- 2 cloves garlic, minced

- 2 teaspoons soy sauce

- 1 pinch ground black pepper to taste

DIRECTIONS

1. Melt the butter in skillet over medium heat; add the mushrooms; cook and stir until the mushrooms have softened and released their liquid, about 5 minutes. Stir in the garlic; continue to cook and stir for 1 minute. Pour in the soy sauce; cook the mushrooms in the soy sauce until the liquid has evaporated, about 4 minutes.

BAKED LEMON CHICKEN WITH MUSHROOM SAUCE

Servings: 6 | Prep: 15m | Cooks: 40m | Total: 55m

NUTRITION FACTS

Calories: 240.3 | Carbohydrates: 5.2g | Protein: 26.3g | Cholesterol: 87.9mg | Sodium: 195.7mg

INGREDIENTS

- 1 tablespoon olive oil

- 6 skinless, boneless chicken breast halves

- 1 lemon

- 1/4 cup butter

- 3 cups fresh sliced mushrooms

- 2 tablespoons all-purpose flour

- 1/2 cup chicken broth, or more as needed

- 1 tablespoon chopped fresh parsley

DIRECTIONS

1. Preheat oven to 400 degrees F (205 degrees C).
2. Pour olive oil in an 8x8-inch glass baking dish. Place the chicken breasts in the dish, coating each side with oil. Squeeze the juice of 1/2 lemon over each chicken breast. Slice the rest of the lemon and place a lemon slice on top of each chicken piece.
3. Bake in the preheated oven until no longer pink in the center and the juices run clear, 30 to 40 minutes. An instant-read thermometer inserted into the center should read at least 165 degrees F (74 degrees C).

4. Melt butter in a skillet over medium heat; add mushrooms. Cook and stir until mushrooms are brown and liquid is evaporated, about 6 minutes. Sprinkle flour over mushrooms and stir until coated. Add chicken broth, stirring to make a medium-thick sauce. Allow sauce to reduce, adjusting with a little more broth to make a creamy sauce. Add fresh parsley at the last minute. Spoon the sauce over the baked chicken breasts.

SLOW COOKER CHICKEN CACCIATORE

Servings: 6 | Prep: 15m | Cooks: 9h | Total: 9h15m

NUTRITION FACTS

Calories: 260.6 | Carbohydrates: 23.7g | Protein: 27.1g | Cholesterol: 63.4mg | Sodium: 589.8mg

INGREDIENTS

- 6 skinless, boneless chicken breast halves
- 1 (28 ounce) jar spaghetti sauce
- 2 green bell pepper, seeded and cubed
- 8 ounces fresh mushrooms, sliced
- 1 onion, finely diced
- 2 tablespoons minced garlic

DIRECTIONS

1. Put the chicken in the slow cooker. Top with the spaghetti sauce, green bell peppers, mushrooms, onion, and garlic.
2. Cover, and cook on Low for 7 to 9 hours.

ALICE CHICKEN

Servings: 4 | Prep: 5m | Cooks: 15m | Total: 1h20m | Additional: 1h

NUTRITION FACTS

Calories: 929.8 | Carbohydrates: 31.9g | Protein: 46.8g | Cholesterol: 152.3mg | Sodium: 1974.6mg

INGREDIENTS

- 4 skinless, boneless chicken breast halves
- 5 fluid ounces Worcestershire sauce
- 8 slices bacon
- 8 ounces fresh mushrooms, sliced
- 1 (8 ounce) package Monterey Jack cheese, shredded
- 1 (16 ounce) container honey mustard salad dressing

* 2 tablespoons butter

DIRECTIONS

1. Place chicken in a glass dish or bowl; poke with a fork several times, then pour Worcestershire sauce in and turn to coat. Cover dish or bowl and refrigerate for about 1 hour.
2. Place bacon in a large, deep skillet. Cook over medium high heat until evenly brown. Drain, and set aside.
3. Heat butter in a small skillet over medium heat. Add mushrooms, and saute for about 10 minutes, or until soft; set aside.
4. Preheat oven to Broil.
5. Remove chicken from marinade (discard any remaining liquid), and broil for about 5 minutes each side. When chicken is almost finished, top each breast with 2 slices bacon, then cheese. Continue to broil until cheese has melted, then remove from oven. Serve with mushrooms and salad dressing for topping.

CHICKEN WILD RICE SOUP
Servings: 8 | Prep: 15m | Cooks: 2h10m | Total: 2h25m

NUTRITION FACTS

Calories: 528.6 | Carbohydrates: 28.7g | Protein: 32.7g | Cholesterol: 97.3mg | Sodium: 1514.2mg

INGREDIENTS

* 1/2cup butter
* 1 finely chopped onion
* 1/2cup chopped celery
* 1/2cup sliced carrots
* 1/2pound fresh sliced mushrooms
* 3/4 cup all-purpose flour
* 6 cups chicken broth
* 2 cups cooked wild rice
* 1 pound boneless skinless chicken breasts, cooked and cubed

* 1/2teaspoon salt
* 1/2teaspoon curry powder
* 1/2teaspoon mustard powder
* 1/2teaspoon dried parsley
* 1/2 teaspoon ground black pepper
* 1 cup slivered almonds
* 3 tablespoons dry sherry
* 2 cups half-and-half

DIRECTIONS

1. Melt butter in a large saucepan over medium heat. Stir in the onion, celery and carrots and saute for 5 minutes. Add the mushrooms and saute for 2 more minutes. Then add the flour and stir well. Gradually pour in the chicken broth, stirring constantly, until all has been added. Bring just to a boil, reduce heat to low and let simmer.
2. Next, add the rice, chicken, salt, curry powder, mustard powder, parsley, ground black pepper, almonds and sherry. Allow to heat through, then pour in the half-and-half. Let simmer for 1 to 2 hours. (Note: Do not boil or your roux will break.)

REAL ITALIAN CALZONES

Servings: 8 | Prep: 1h | Cooks: 30m | Total: 1h30m

NUTRITION FACTS

Calories: 334.6 | Carbohydrates: 31.6g | Protein: 13.8g | Cholesterol: 63.6mg | Sodium: 667mg

INGREDIENTS

- 1 (.25 ounce) package active dry yeast
- 1 cup warm water
- 1 tablespoon olive oil
- 1 teaspoon white sugar
- 1 teaspoon salt
- 2 1/2 cups all-purpose flour, divided
- 1 teaspoon olive oil
- 1/2 cup ricotta cheese
- 1 1/2 cups shredded Cheddar cheese
- 1/2 cup diced pepperoni
- 1/2 cup sliced fresh mushrooms
- 1 tablespoon dried basil leaves
- 1 egg, beaten

DIRECTIONS

1. To Make Dough: In a small bowl, dissolve yeast in water. Add the oil, sugar and salt; mix in 1 cup of the flour until smooth. Gradually stir in the rest of the flour, until dough is smooth and workable. Knead dough on a lightly floured surface for about 5 minutes, or until it is elastic. Lay dough in a bowl containing 1 teaspoon olive oil, then flip the dough, cover and let rise for 40 minutes, or until almost doubled.
2. To Make Filling: While dough is rising, combine the ricotta cheese, Cheddar cheese, pepperoni, mushrooms and basil leaves in a large bowl. Mix well, cover bowl and refrigerate to chill.
3. Preheat oven to 375 degrees F (190 degrees C).

4. When dough is ready, punch it down and separate it into 2 equal parts. Roll parts out into thin circles on a lightly floured surface. Fill each circle with 1/2 of the cheese/meat filling and fold over, securing edges by folding in and pressing with a fork. Brush the top of each calzone with egg and place on a lightly greased cookie sheet.

5. Bake at 375 degrees F (190 degrees C) for 30 minutes. Serve hot.

PORTOBELLO PENNE PASTA CASSEROLE

Servings: 8 | Prep: 15m | Cooks: 30m | Total: 45m

NUTRITION FACTS

Calories: 380 | Carbohydrates: 32.1g | Fat: 21.3g | Protein: 16g | Cholesterol: 23mg | Sodium: 811mg

INGREDIENTS

- 1 (8 ounce) package uncooked penne pasta
- 2 tablespoons vegetable oil
- 1/2 pound portobello mushrooms, thinly sliced
- 1/2 cup margarine
- 1/4 cup all-purpose flour
- 1 large clove garlic, minced
- 1/2 teaspoon dried basil
- 2 cups milk
- 2 cups shredded mozzarella cheese
- 1 (10 ounce) package frozen chopped spinach, thawed
- 1/4 cup soy sauce

DIRECTIONS

1. Preheat oven to 350 degrees F (175 degrees C). Lightly grease a 9x13 inch baking dis

2. Bring a large pot of lightly salted water to a boil. Place pasta in the pot, cook for 8 to 10 minutes, until al dente, and drain.

3. Heat the oil in a saucepan over medium heat. Stir in the mushrooms, cook 1 minute, and set aside. Melt margarine in the saucepan. Mix in flour, garlic, and basil. Gradually mix in milk until thickened. Stir in 1 cup cheese until melted. Remove saucepan from heat, and mix in cooked pasta, mushrooms, spinach, and soy sauce. Transfer to the prepared baking dish, and top with remaining cheese.

4. Bake 20 minutes in the preheated oven, until bubbly and lightly brown.

GRANDMA'S CHICKEN CHARDON

Servings: 8 | Prep: 10m | Cooks: 45m | Total: 55m

NUTRITION FACTS

Calories: 280.6 | Carbohydrates: 13g | Protein: 30.3g | Cholesterol: 110.1mg | Sodium: 334.1mg

INGREDIENTS

- 8 skinless, boneless chicken breast halves
- 1 egg
- 1 dash salt and pepper to taste
- 2 teaspoons garlic powder, divided
- 1 cup bread crumbs
- 1/2 cup grated Parmesan cheese
- 1 pound sliced fresh mushrooms
- 1/4 cup butter, melted
- 1 tablespoon fresh lemon juice
- 1 teaspoon chopped fresh parsley

DIRECTIONS

1. Preheat the oven to 375 degrees F (190 degrees C).
2. In a shallow bowl, beat the egg with salt, pepper and 1 teaspoon garlic powder. In a separate dish, mix bread crumbs with 1 teaspoon of garlic powder and Parmesan cheese. Set aside.
3. Mix together the melted butter and lemon juice. Pour about 2/3 of the butter mixture into the bottom of a 9x13 inch baking dish. Tilt pan to coat the bottom. Spread mushrooms in an even layer in the bottom of the dish. Dip each chicken breast into the egg mixture, then into the bread crumb mixture. Place on top of the mushrooms. Drizzle remaining butter over the chicken, and sprinkle with parsley.
4. Bake uncovered for 45 minutes in the preheated oven, until chicken is golden brown and juices run clear.

BEEF STROGANOFF FOR INSTANT POT

Servings: 8 | Prep: 20m | Cooks: 37m | Total: 1h2m | Additional: 5m

NUTRITION FACTS

Calories: 535.9 | Carbohydrates: 45.2g | Protein: 29g | Cholesterol: 121.4mg | Sodium: 1312.5mg

INGREDIENTS

- 2 tablespoons canola oil
- 1/2 onion, diced
- 2 tablespoons soy sauce
- 3 cups chopped mushrooms

- 2 teaspoons salt, divided
- 2 pounds beef stew meat, cut into 1-inch cubes
- 1 teaspoon freshly ground black pepper
- 3 cloves garlic, minced
- 1/2 teaspoon dried thyme
- 2 tablespoons all-purpose flour
- 3 cups chicken broth
- 1 (16 ounce) package wide egg noodles
- 3/4 cup sour cream, or to taste

DIRECTIONS

1. Turn on a multi-cooker (such as Instant Pot®) and select Saute function. Heat oil for 1 minute. Add onion and 1/2 teaspoon salt; cook and stir until onion begins to soften, 3 to 4 minutes.
2. Season beef with 1 teaspoon salt and pepper. Add to the pot. Cook and stir until browned evenly on all sides, about 2 minutes. Add garlic and thyme; cook until fragrant, about 30 seconds. Pour in soy sauce.
3. Stir mushrooms into the pot. Stir in flour until evenly incorporated. Pour in chicken broth and remaining 1/2 teaspoon salt. Close and lock the lid. Set timer for 10 minutes. Set to high pressure according to manufacturer's instructions, 10 to 15 minutes.
4. Release pressure carefully using the quick-release method. Open pressure cooker; stir in egg noodles. Seal and bring to high pressure again, about 5 minutes; cook for 5 minutes.
5. Release pressure naturally according to manufacturer's instruction for 5 minutes. Release remaining pressure using the quick-release method. Open pressure cooker; stir in sour cream.

CHICKEN TETRAZZINI

Servings: 4 | Prep: 15m | Cooks: 45m | Total: 1h

NUTRITION FACTS

Calories: 730.4 | Carbohydrates: 52.7g | Protein: 33.1g | Cholesterol: 173.3mg | Sodium: 919mg

INGREDIENTS

- 1 (8 ounce) package spaghetti, broken into pieces
- 1/4cup butter
- 1/4cup all-purpose flour
- 3/4 teaspoon salt
- 1 cup heavy cream
- 2 tablespoons sherry
- 1 (4.5 ounce) can sliced mushrooms, drained
- 2 cups chopped cooked chicken

- 1/4 teaspoon ground black pepper
- 1 cup chicken broth
- 1/2 cup grated Parmesan cheese
- 1 cup heavy cream

DIRECTIONS

1. Preheat oven to 350 degrees F (175 degrees C). Lightly grease a 9x13 inch baking dish.
2. Bring a large pot of lightly salted water to a boil. Add spaghetti, and cook for 8 to 10 minutes, or until al dente; drain.
3. Meanwhile, in a large saucepan, melt butter over low heat. Stir in flour, salt, and pepper. Cook, stirring, until smooth. Remove from heat, and gradually stir in chicken broth and cream.
4. Return to heat, and bring to a low boil for 1 minute, stirring constantly. Add sherry, then stir in cooked spaghetti, mushrooms, and chicken. Pour mixture into the prepared baking dish, and top with Parmesan cheese.
5. Bake 30 minutes in the preheated oven, until bubbly and lightly browned.

EASIER CHICKEN MARSALA

Servings: 4 | Prep: 10m | Cooks: 20m | Total: 30m

NUTRITION FACTS

Calories: 286 | Carbohydrates: 11.4g | Protein: 27.9g | Cholesterol: 79.6mg | Sodium: 313.4mg

INGREDIENTS

- 1/4 cup all-purpose flour
- 1/2 teaspoon garlic salt
- 1/4 teaspoon ground black pepper
- 1/2 teaspoon dried oregano
- 4 boneless, skinless chicken breast halves
- 1 tablespoon olive oil
- 1 tablespoon butter
- 1 cup sliced fresh mushrooms
- 1/2 cup Marsala wine

DIRECTIONS

1. In a medium bowl, stir together the flour, garlic salt, pepper, and oregano. Dredge chicken in the mixture to lightly coat.
2. Heat olive oil and butter in a large skillet over medium heat. Fry the chicken in the skillet for 2 minutes, or until lightly browned on one side. Turn chicken over, and add mushrooms. Cook about 2 minutes, until other side of chicken is lightly browned. Stir mushrooms so that they cook evenly.

3. Pour Marsala wine over the chicken. Cover skillet, and reduce heat to low; simmer for 10 minutes, or until chicken is no longer pink and juices run clear.

PORK MARSALA

Servings: 4 | Prep: 10m | Cooks: 20m | Total: 30m

NUTRITION FACTS

Calories: 455 | Carbohydrates: 18.3g | Fat: 27.6g | Protein: 17.6g | Cholesterol: 61mg | Sodium: 356mg

INGREDIENTS

- 1/3 cup all-purpose flour
- 1/4 teaspoon salt
- 1/4 teaspoon garlic salt
- 3/4 teaspoon garlic powder
- 1/2 teaspoon dried oregano
- 1 pound boneless pork loin chops, pounded thin
- 3 tablespoons butter
- 1/4 cup olive oil
- 2 cups sliced fresh mushrooms
- 1 teaspoon minced garlic
- 1 cup Marsala wine

DIRECTIONS

1. Mix flour, salt ,garlic salt, garlic powder, and oregano together in a medium bowl. Add pork chops, and toss until well coated.
2. Heat butter and olive oil in a large skillet over medium heat. Place pork in skillet in a single layer, and cook, turning occasionally, until brown on both sides. Add mushrooms and minced garlic; cook and stir briefly.
3. Stir in wine, scraping the skillet to loosen any brown bits. Cover and simmer over medium heat until pork is tender and sauce is thickened, about 15 minutes. If sauce is too thick, adjust by stirring in a small amount of wine.

SCRUMPTIOUS SALISBURY STEAK IN MUSHROOM GRAVY

Servings: 6 | Prep: 10m | Cooks: 25m | Total: 35m

NUTRITION FACTS

Calories: 296.2 | Carbohydrates: 12.6g | Protein: 19.4g | Cholesterol: 102mg | Sodium: 950.5mg

INGREDIENTS

- 1 pound ground beef
- 1 egg
- 3 tablespoons crushed buttery round cracker crumbs
- 2 tablespoons finely chopped onion
- 1/2 teaspoon salt
- 1/2 teaspoon pepper
- 1/4 teaspoon poultry seasoning
- 2 (4 ounce) cans sliced mushrooms with juice
- 3 tablespoons butter
- 3 tablespoons all-purpose flour
- 3 cups milk
- 3 cubes beef bouillon

DIRECTIONS

1. In a medium bowl, mix together the ground beef, egg, cracker crumbs, onion, salt, pepper and poultry seasoning using your hands. Shape into 6 patties about 1 inch thick.
2. Fry the patties in a large skillet over medium-high heat for 3 to 4 minutes per side, or until browned. Drain off grease, and remove patties to a platter; keep warm.
3. Melt the butter in the same skillet, and add the mushrooms. Cook and stir for about 2 minutes. Sprinkle the flour over, and mix in until blended. Stir in the milk and beef bouillon. Cook and stir over medium heat until smooth and starting to thicken. Return the patties to the gravy and cook over low heat, uncovered, for 10 minutes, stirring occasionally.

MUSHROOM CHICKEN PICCATA
Servings: 6 | Prep: 20m | Cooks: 30m | Total: 50m

NUTRITION FACTS

Calories: 287.7 | Carbohydrates: 12.6g | Protein: 31.1g | Cholesterol: 121mg | Sodium: 696.6mg

INGREDIENTS

- 1/2 cup all-purpose flour
- 1 teaspoon salt
- 1/2 teaspoon paprika
- 1 egg
- 2 tablespoons milk
- 1/2 pound fresh mushrooms, sliced
- 1/4 cup chopped onion
- 1 cup chicken broth
- 1/2 cup white wine
- 2 tablespoons lemon juice

- 6 skinless, boneless chicken breast halves
- 4 tablespoons butter
- 1 tablespoon cornstarch
- 1 tablespoon chopped fresh parsley, for garnis

DIRECTIONS

1. In a shallow dish or bowl, mix together flour, salt and paprika. In a separate dish or bowl, mix together egg and milk. Dip chicken pieces in egg mixture, then in seasoned flour.
2. In a large skillet, heat butter or margarine over medium-high heat. Saute chicken pieces until golden brown. Add mushrooms and onion and saute for 3 to 5 minutes.
3. In a medium bowl combine the broth, wine, lemon juice and cornstarch. Mix together and pour mixture over chicken and mushrooms. Reduce heat to medium low and let chicken mixture simmer for 25 minutes or until chicken is cooked through and juices run clear. Sprinkle with parsley and serve.

MANICOTTI ITALIAN CASSEROLE

Servings: 8 | Prep: 10m | Cooks: 30m | Total: 40m

NUTRITION FACTS

Calories: 909 | Carbohydrates: 77.6g | Protein: 52.1g | Cholesterol: 126.8mg | Sodium: 2247.8mg

INGREDIENTS

- 1 pound rigatoni pasta
- 1 pound ground beef
- 1 pound Italian sausage
- 1 (8 ounce) can mushrooms, drained
- 2 (32 ounce) jars spaghetti sauce
- 1 1/2 pounds shredded mozzarella cheese
- 1 (3 ounce) package thinly sliced pepperoni

DIRECTIONS

1. Preheat oven to 350 degrees F (175 degrees C).
2. Bring a large pot of lightly salted water to boil. Pour in rigatoni, and cook until al dente, about 8 to 10 minutes. Drain, and set pasta aside.
3. Meanwhile, brown ground beef and italian sausage in a large skillet over medium heat. With a slotted spoon, remove beef and sausage to a baking dish. Stir mushrooms, spaghetti sauce, and cooked pasta into the baking dish. Sprinkle cheese and pepperoni over the top.
4. Bake in preheated oven until the cheese is brown and bubbly, about 20 minutes.

GREEN BEAN AND MUSHROOM MEDLEY

Servings: 6 | Prep: 20m | Cooks: 15m | Total: 35m

NUTRITION FACTS

Calories: 102.9 | Carbohydrates: 7.7g | Protein: 1.9g | Cholesterol: 20.3mg | Sodium: 610mg

INGREDIENTS

- 1/2 pound fresh green beans, cut into 1-inch lengths
- 2 carrots, cut into thick strips
- 1/4 cup butter
- 1 onion, sliced
- 1/2 pound fresh mushrooms, sliced

- 1 teaspoon salt
- 1/2 teaspoon seasoned salt
- 1/4 teaspoon garlic salt
- 1/4 teaspoon white pepper

DIRECTIONS

1. Place green beans and carrots in 1 inch of boiling water. Cover, and cook until tender but still firm. Drain.
2. Melt butter in a large skillet over medium heat. Saute onions and mushrooms until almost tender. Reduce heat, cover, and simmer 3 minutes. Stir in green beans, carrots, salt, seasoned salt, garlic salt, and white pepper. Cover, and cook for 5 minutes over medium heat.

AMAZING ITALIAN LEMON BUTTER CHICKEN

Servings: 6 | Prep: 10m | Cooks: 20m | Total: 30m

NUTRITION FACTS

Calories: 659.6 | Carbohydrates: 37.4g | Protein: 26.8g | Cholesterol: 155mg | Sodium: 660.3mg

INGREDIENTS

- 1/4 cup white wine
- 5 tablespoons fresh lemon juice
- 5 tablespoons heavy cream
- 1 cup butter, chilled

- 1 tablespoon butter
- 1/4 cup all-purpose flour
- 1/2 pinch salt and pepper to taste
- 4 ounces bacon

- 1 pinch salt and pepper to taste
- 1/2 pound dry farfalle (bow tie) pasta
- 4 skinless, boneless chicken breast halves - pounded to 1/4 inch thickness
- 1 tablespoon olive oil

- 6 ounces mushrooms, sliced
- 6 ounces artichoke hearts, drained and halved
- 2 teaspoons capers, drained

- 1/4 cup chopped fresh parsley for garnish

DIRECTIONS

1. To make the sauce, pour the wine and lemon juice into a saucepan over medium heat. Cook at a low boil until the liquid is reduced by 1/3. Stir in cream, and simmer until it thickens. Gradually add the butter 1 tablespoon at a time to the sauce, stirring until completely incorporated. Season with salt and pepper. Remove from heat, and keep warm.

2. Bring a large pot of lightly salted water to boil. Add pasta, and cook until al dente, about 8 to 10 minutes. Drain, and set aside.

3. To make the chicken, heat oil and 2 tablespoons butter in a large skillet over medium heat. In a bowl, stir together flour, salt, and pepper. Lightly coat chicken with flour mixture. Without crowding, carefully place chicken in hot oil. (If necessary, cook in batches.) Fry until cooked through and golden brown on both sides. Remove the chicken to paper towels. Stir the bacon, mushrooms, artichokes, and capers into the oil; cook until the mushrooms are soft.

4. Cut the chicken breasts into bite-size strips, and return them to the skillet. Stir half of the lemon butter sauce into the chicken mixture.

5. To serve, place pasta in a large bowl. Stir the chicken mixture into the pasta. Taste, and adjust seasonings. Stir in additional lemon butter sauce as desired. Toss well, and garnish with parsley.

SIRLOIN TIPS AND MUSHROOMS

Servings: 6 | Prep: 15m | Cooks: 45m | Total: 1h5m | Additional: 15m

NUTRITION FACTS

Calories: 257 | Carbohydrates: 7.1g | Protein: 21.7g | Cholesterol: 49.1mg | Sodium: 555.5mg

INGREDIENTS

- 3 tablespoons olive oil
- 3 cloves garlic, minced
- 1 1/2 pounds beef sirloin

- 1 (8 ounce) can tomato sauce
- salt to taste
- freshly ground pepper, to taste

- 1 (16 ounce) can mushrooms, with liquid
- 3/4 cup red wine

DIRECTIONS

1. Cut beef into cubes. In a large skillet over medium/high heat, heat the olive oil and brown beef cubes with the garlic.
2. Add mushrooms with liquid, tomato sauce, salt, pepper and red wine. Cook for 30 minutes or until beef cubes are tender. Add a little more wine while cooking if desired.

SENSATIONAL SIRLOIN KABOBS

Servings: 8 | Prep: 15m | Cooks: 15m | Total: 8h30m | Additional: 8h

NUTRITION FACTS

Calories: 326.5 | Carbohydrates: 19.2g | Protein: 24g | Cholesterol: 76mg | Sodium: 608mg

INGREDIENTS

- 1/4 cup soy sauce
- 3 tablespoons light brown sugar
- 3 tablespoons distilled white vinegar
- 1/2 teaspoon garlic powder
- 1/2 teaspoon seasoned salt
- 1/2 teaspoon garlic pepper seasoning
- 4 fluid ounces lemon-lime flavored carbonated beverage
- 2 pounds beef sirloin steak, cut into 1 1/2 inch cubes
- 2 green bell peppers, cut into 2 inch pieces
- 4 eaches skewers
- 1/2 pound fresh mushrooms, stems removed
- 1 pint cherry tomatoes
- 1 fresh pineapple - peeled, cored and cubed

DIRECTIONS

1. In a medium bowl, mix soy sauce, light brown sugar, distilled white vinegar, garlic powder, seasoned salt, garlic pepper seasoning, and lemon-lime flavored carbonated beverage. Reserve about 1/2 cup of this marinade for basting. Place steak in a large resealable plastic bag. Cover with the remaining marinade, and seal. Refrigerate for 8 hours, or overnight.
2. Bring a saucepan of water to a boil. Add green peppers, and cook for 1 minute, just to blanch. Drain, and set aside.

3. Preheat grill for high heat. Thread steak, green peppers, mushrooms, tomatoes, and pineapple onto skewers in an alternating fashion. Discard marinade and the bag.
4. Lightly oil the grill grate. Cook kabobs on the prepared grill for 10 minutes, or to desired doneness. Baste frequently with reserved marinade during the last 5 minutes of cooking.

SUPERB SAUTEED MUSHROOMS

Servings: 4 | Prep: 10m | Cooks: 15m | Total: 25m

NUTRITION FACTS

Calories: 199.2 | Carbohydrates: 5.3g | Protein: 3.9g | Cholesterol: 22.9mg | Sodium: 375.7mg

INGREDIENTS

- 3 tablespoons olive oil
- 3 tablespoons butter
- 1 pound button mushrooms, sliced
- 1 clove garlic, thinly sliced
- 1 tablespoon red cooking wine
- 1 tablespoon teriyaki sauce, or more to taste
- 1/4 teaspoon garlic salt, or to taste
- 1 pinch freshly ground black pepper to taste

DIRECTIONS

1. Heat olive oil and butter in a large saucepan over medium heat. Cook and stir mushrooms, garlic, cooking wine, teriyaki sauce, garlic salt, and black pepper in the hot oil and butter until mushrooms are lightly browned, about 5 minutes. Reduce heat to low and simmer until mushrooms are tender, 5 to 8 more minutes.

NO-NOODLE ZUCCHINI LASAGNA

Servings: 8 | Prep: 30m | Cooks: 1h | Total: 1h30m

NUTRITION FACTS

Calories: 494 | Carbohydrates: 23.2g | Protein: 41.3g | Cholesterol: 117.7mg | Sodium: 2199.7mg

INGREDIENTS

- 2 large zucchini
- 1 tablespoon salt
- 1 pound ground beef
- 1 tablespoon chopped fresh oregano
- 1/4 cup hot water as needed
- 1 egg

- 1 1/2 teaspoons ground black pepper
- 1 small green bell pepper, diced
- 1 onion, diced
- 1 cup tomato paste
- 1 (16 ounce) can tomato sauce
- 1/4 cup red wine
- 1 (15 ounce) container low-fat ricotta cheese
- 2 tablespoons chopped fresh parsley
- 1 (16 ounce) package frozen chopped spinach, thawed and drained
- 1 pound fresh mushrooms, sliced
- 8 ounces shredded mozzarella cheese

DIRECTIONS

1. Preheat oven to 325 degrees F (165 degrees C). Grease a deep 9x13 inch baking pan.
2. Slice zucchini lengthwise into very thin slices. Sprinkle slices lightly with salt; set aside to drain in a colander.
3. To prepare the meat sauce, cook and stir ground beef and black pepper in a large skillet over medium high heat for 5 minutes. Add in green pepper and onion; cook and stir until meat is no longer pink. Stir in tomato paste, tomato sauce, wine, basil, and oregano, adding a small amount of hot water if sauce is too thick. Bring to a boil; reduce heat and simmer sauce for about 20 minutes, stirring frequently.
4. Meanwhile, stir egg, ricotta, and parsley together in a bowl until well combined.
5. To assemble lasagna, spread 1/2 of the meat sauce into the bottom of prepared pan. Then layer 1/2 the zucchini slices, 1/2 the ricotta mixture, all of the spinach, followed by all of the mushrooms, then 1/2 the mozzarella cheese. Repeat by layering the remaining meat sauce, zucchini slices, ricotta mixture, and mozzarella. Spread Parmesan cheese evenly over the top; cover with foil.
6. Bake for 45 minutes. Remove foil; raise oven temperature to 350 degrees F (175 degrees C), and bake an additional 15 minutes. Let stand for 5 minutes before serving.

MUSHROOM RICE

Servings: 4 | Prep: 5m | Cooks: 25m | Total: 30m

NUTRITION FACTS

Calories: 215.7 | Carbohydrates: 41.1g | Protein: 5.3g | Cholesterol: 8.4mg | Sodium: 1181.1mg

INGREDIENTS

- 2 teaspoons butter
- 6 mushrooms, coarsely chopped
- 2 cups chicken broth
- 1 cup uncooked white rice

- 1 clove garlic, minced

- 1 green onion, finely chopped

- 1/2 teaspoon chopped fresh parsley

- 1 teaspoon salt and pepper to taste

DIRECTIONS

1. Melt butter in a saucepan over medium heat. Cook mushrooms, garlic and green onion until mushrooms are cooked and liquid has evaporated. Stir in chicken broth and rice. Season with parsley, salt and pepper. Reduce heat, cover and simmer for 20 minutes.

PORTOBELLO MUSHROOM STROGANOFF

Servings: 4 | Prep: 10m | Cooks: 20m | Total: 30m

NUTRITION FACTS

Calories: 525.2 | Carbohydrates: 53.3g | Protein: 12.8g | Cholesterol: 101.4mg | Sodium: 295.4mg

INGREDIENTS

- 3 tablespoons butter

- 1 large onion, chopped

- 3/4 pound portobello mushrooms, sliced

- 1 1/2 cups vegetable broth

- 1 1/2 cups sour cream

- 3 tablespoons all-purpose flour

- 1/4 cup chopped fresh parsley

- 8 ounces dried egg noodles

DIRECTIONS

1. Bring a large pot of lightly salted water to a boil. Add egg noodles, and cook until al dente, about 7 minutes. Remove from heat, drain, and set aside.
2. At the same time, melt butter in a large heavy skillet over medium heat. Add onion, and cook, stirring until softened. Turn the heat up to medium-high, and add sliced mushrooms. Cook until the mushrooms are limp and browned. Remove to a bowl, and set aside.
3. In the same skillet, stir in vegetable broth, being sure to stir in any browned bits off the bottom of the pan. Bring to a boil, and cook until the mixture has reduced by 1/3. Reduce heat to low, and return the mushrooms and onion to the skillet.
4. Remove the pan from the heat, stir together the sour cream and flour; then blend into the mushrooms. Return the skillet to the burner, and continue cooking over low heat, just until the sauce thickens. Stir in the parsley, and season to taste with salt and pepper. Serve over cooked egg noodles.

CLASSIC BEEF STROGANOFF

Servings: 8 | Prep: 15m | Cooks: 1h30m | Total: 1h45m

NUTRITION FACTS

Calories: 307 | Carbohydrates: 4.1g | Fat: 24.5g | Protein: 15.8g | Cholesterol: 86mg | Sodium: 288mg

INGREDIENTS

- 1 tablespoon vegetable oil
- 2 pounds beef chuck roast, cut into 1/2-inch thick strips
- salt and pepper to taste
- 1 tablespoon butter
- 1/2 medium onion, sliced or diced
- 8 ounces sliced mushrooms
- 2 cloves garlic, minced
- 1 1/2 tablespoons all-purpose flour
- 1/2 cup white wine
- 2 cups beef broth, divided
- 3/4 cup creme fraiche
- 1 tablespoon fresh chopped chives
- salt and pepper to taste

DIRECTIONS

1. Season beef generously with salt and pepper.
2. Heat oil in a large skillet over high heat until nearly smoking. Stir in beef; cook, stirring constantly, for 6-7 minutes, until liquid evaporates and meat browns. Remove meat from the pan and set aside.
3. Stir butter, mushrooms and onions into the pan; cook and stir over medium heat until the vegetables are lightly browned. Add garlic and stir for 30 seconds. Stir in flour; cook for 1-2 minutes until incorporated.
4. Stir in wine and 1 cup of stock, scraping the bottom of the pan to release any browned bits. Bring to a simmer, cook for 3-4 minutes, until the sauce thickens.
5. Return beef to the pan. Stir in remaining cup of stock; bring to a simmer and cook on low heat for about 1 hour with the lid on, until the beef is tender and the sauce is thick. Stir every 20 minutes.
6. Stir in creme fraiche. Stir in chives. Season with salt and pepper to taste.

GARY'S STUFFED MUSHROOMS

Servings: 12 | Prep: 30m | Cooks: 12m | Total: 42m

NUTRITION FACTS

Calories: 413.1 | Carbohydrates: 14.4g | Protein: 5.9g | Cholesterol: 105.7mg | Sodium: 693.5mg

INGREDIENTS

- 12 large fresh mushrooms, stems removed
- 1 (6 ounce) package chicken flavored dry stuffing mix
- 1 (8 ounce) package cream cheese, softened
- 1/2 pound imitation crabmeat, flaked
- 2 cups butter
- 2 cloves garlic, peeled and minced
- salt and pepper to taste
- garlic powder to taste
- crushed red pepper to taste

DIRECTIONS

1. Arrange mushroom caps on a medium baking sheet, bottoms up. Chop and reserve mushroom stems.
2. Prepare chicken flavored dry stuffing mix according to package directions.
3. Preheat oven to 350 degrees F (175 degrees C).
4. In a medium saucepan over medium heat, melt butter. Mix in garlic and cook until tender, about 5 minutes.
5. In a medium bowl, mix together reserved mushroom stems, prepared dry stuffing mix, cream cheese and imitation crabmeat. Liberally stuff mushrooms with the mixture. Drizzle with the butter and garlic. Season with salt, pepper, garlic powder and crushed red pepper.
6. Bake uncovered in the preheated oven 10 to 12 minutes, or until stuffing is lightly browned.

CHICKEN AND MUSHROOMS

Servings: 2 | Prep: 10m | Cooks: 30m | Total: 40m

NUTRITION FACTS

Calories: 397.8 | Carbohydrates: 3.7g | Protein: 28.1g | Cholesterol: 90.8mg | Sodium: 355.4mg

INGREDIENTS

- 2 chicken breast halves, boneless, skin-on
- 1 pinch salt and ground black pepper to taste
- 2 tablespoons olive oil
- 8 ounces fresh mushrooms, sliced 1/4 inch thick
- 1 pinch salt
- 1/2 cup water
- 1 tablespoon butter
- 1 pinch salt and ground black pepper to taste

DIRECTIONS

1. Preheat oven to 400 degrees F (200 degrees C).
2. Season chicken on all sides with salt and ground black pepper.
3. Heat olive oil over medium-high heat in an ovenproof skillet. Place chicken skin-side down in skillet and cook until browned, about 5 minutes.
4. Turn chicken over; stir mushrooms with a pinch of salt into skillet. Increase heat to high; cook, stirring mushrooms occasionally, until mushrooms shrink slightly, about 5 minutes.
5. Transfer skillet to the preheated oven and cook until chicken is no longer pink in the center and the juices run clear, 15 to 20 minutes. An instant-read thermometer inserted into the center should read 165 degrees F (74 degrees C). Transfer chicken breasts to a plate and loosely tent with foil; set aside.
6. Set skillet on the stovetop over medium-high heat; cook and stir mushrooms until brown bits start to form on the bottom of the pan, about 5 minutes. Pour water into the skillet, and bring to a boil while scraping the browned bits off of the bottom of the pan. Cook until water is reduced by half, about 2 minutes. Remove from heat.
7. Stir in any accumulated juices from the chicken into the skillet. Stir butter into mushroom mixture, stirring constantly until butter is completely melted and incorporated.
8. Season with salt and pepper. Spoon mushroom sauce over chicken and serve.

CHICKEN MARSALA

Servings: 2 | Prep: 20m | Cooks: 40m | Total: 1h

NUTRITION FACTS

Calories: 798.7 | Carbohydrates: 26.8g | Protein: 51.1g | Cholesterol: 185.4mg | Sodium: 2390.8mg

INGREDIENTS

- 2 eaches skin-on, boneless chicken breast halves
- 1 teaspoon salt and ground black pepper to taste
- 3 tablespoons butter, divided
- 2 tablespoons olive oil
- 5 white mushrooms, sliced
- 1 shallot, minced
- 1 tablespoon all-purpose flour
- 1 cup Marsala wine
- 2 cups chicken stock
- 2 tablespoons chopped fresh parsley
- 1 teaspoon cold butter

DIRECTIONS

1. Season chicken breasts all over with salt and pepper.
2. Melt 1 1/2 tablespoons butter and olive oil in a skillet over medium heat. Cook chicken breasts, skin-side down, in hot butter and oil until browned, about 5 minutes. Flip and cook until breasts are almost cooked through, about 5 minutes more. Transfer chicken breasts to a plate.
3. Melt 1 1/2 tablespoons butter in the same skillet over medium-high heat. Saute mushrooms with a pinch of salt and a pinch of pepper in hot butter until mushrooms are golden, 5 to 7 minutes. Add minced shallot; cook and stir until softened, 2 to 3 minutes. Sprinkle flour over the top and cook and stir until the bitterness of the flour cooks off, 3 to 4 minutes.
4. Pour wine into skillet and bring to a boil; cook and stir until wine reduces and sauce thickens, 3 to 4 minutes. Add chicken stock; bring to a simmer and cook until slightly reduced, 3 to 5 minutes more.
5. Return chicken breasts to the skillet, reduce heat to low, and cook chicken, turning once, until no longer pink in the center and the juices run clear, about 10 minutes. An instant-read thermometer inserted into the center should read at least 165 degrees F (74 degrees C). Remove from heat.
6. Move chicken to one side of the skillet and tilt the skillet so that the sauce pools at the bottom. Stir parsley and 1 teaspoon cold butter into the sauce, stirring constantly, until sauce is shiny and butter is completely melted. Transfer chicken breasts to plates and spoon mushrooms and sauce over the top.

JAGERSCHNITZEL

Servings: 4 | Prep: 15m | Cooks: 25m | Total: 40m

NUTRITION FACTS

Calories: 555.6 | Carbohydrates: 29.9g | Protein: 32.9g | Cholesterol: 157mg | Sodium: 682.8mg

INGREDIENTS

- 1 cup bread crumbs
- 1 tablespoon all-purpose flour
- salt and pepper to taste
- 2 tablespoons vegetable oil
- 4 raw steak with refuse, 300 g; yields excluding refuses pork steaks or cutlets, pounded thin
- 1 egg, beaten

- 1 medium onion, diced
- 1 (8 ounce) can sliced mushrooms
- 1 1/2 cups water
- 1 cube beef bouillon
- 1 tablespoon cornstarch
- 1/2 cup sour cream

DIRECTIONS

1. In a shallow dish, mix together the bread crumbs and flour. Season with salt and pepper. Place the egg in a separate dish. Heat oil in a large skillet over medium-high heat. Dip pork steaks in egg, then coat with the bread crumb mixture. Fry in the hot oil until browned on both sides and cooked through, about 5 minutes per side.
2. Remove the pork to a platter and keep warm. Add onion and mushrooms to the skillet and cook until lightly browned. Pour in water and dissolve the bouillon cube. Simmer for about 20 minutes. Stir together the cornstarch and sour cream; stir into the skillet. Cook over low heat until thickened but do not boil. Spoon over the pork cutlets and serve immediately.

ROMANTIC CHICKEN WITH ARTICHOKES AND MUSHROOMS

Servings: 4 | Prep: 10m | Cooks: 35m | Total: 45m

NUTRITION FACTS

Calories: 311.9 | Carbohydrates: 9.6g | Protein: 25g | Cholesterol: 74.8mg | Sodium: 426.2mg

INGREDIENTS

- 4 skinless, boneless chicken breast halves
- salt and pepper to taste
- 1 tablespoon olive oil
- 1 tablespoon butter
- 1 (14 ounce) can marinated quartered artichoke hearts, drained, liquid reserved
- 1 cup sliced fresh mushrooms
- 1 cup white wine
- 1 tablespoon capers

DIRECTIONS

1. Season chicken with salt and pepper. Heat oil and butter in a large skillet over medium heat. Brown chicken in oil and butter for 5 to 7 minutes per side; remove from skillet, and set aside.
2. Place artichoke hearts and mushrooms in the skillet, and saute until mushrooms are brown and tender. Return chicken to skillet, and pour in reserved artichoke liquid and wine. Reduce heat to low, and simmer for about 10 to 15 minutes, until chicken is no longer pink and juices run clear.
3. Stir in capers, and simmer for another 5 minutes. Remove from heat; serve immediately.

CLASSIC MEATLOAF

Servings: 10 | Prep: 30m | Cooks: 45m | Total: 1h15m

NUTRITION FACTS

Calories: 284 | Carbohydrates: 14.8g | Fat: 14.9g | Protein: 21.6g | Cholesterol: 85mg | Sodium: 755mg

INGREDIENTS

- 1 carrot, coarsely chopped
- 1 rib celery, coarsely chopped
- 1/2 onion, coarsely chopped
- 1/2 red bell pepper, coarsely chopped
- 4 white mushrooms, coarsely chopped
- 3 cloves garlic, coarsely chopped
- 2 1/2 pounds ground chuck
- 1 tablespoon Worcestershire sauce
- 1 egg, beaten
- 1 teaspoon dried Italian herbs
- 2 teaspoons salt
- 1 teaspoon ground black pepper
- 1/2 teaspoon cayenne pepper
- 1 cup plain bread crumbs
- 1 teaspoon olive oil
- 2 tablespoons brown sugar
- 2 tablespoons ketchup
- 2 tablespoons Dijon mustard
- hot pepper sauce to taste

DIRECTIONS

1. Preheat the oven to 325 degrees F.
2. Place the carrot, celery, onion, red bell pepper, mushrooms, and garlic in a food processor, and pulse until very finely chopped, almost to a puree. Place the minced vegetables into a large mixing bowl, and mix in ground chuck, Worcestershire sauce, and egg. Add Italian herbs, salt, black pepper, and cayenne pepper. Mix gently with a wooden spoon to incorporate vegetables and egg into the meat. Pour in bread crumbs. With your hand, gently mix in the crumbs with your fingertips just until combined, about 1 minute.
3. Form the meatloaf into a ball. Pour olive oil into a baking dish and place the ball of meat into the dish. Shape the ball into a loaf, about 4 inches high by 6 inches across.
4. Bake in the preheated oven just until the meatloaf is hot, about 15 minutes.
5. Meanwhile, in a small bowl, mix together brown sugar, ketchup, Dijon mustard, and hot sauce. Stir until the brown sugar has dissolved.
6. Remove the meatloaf from the oven. With the back of a spoon, smooth the glaze onto the top of the meatloaf, then pull a little bit of glaze down the sides of the meatloaf with the back of the spoon.

7. Return meatloaf to oven, and bake until the loaf is no longer pink inside and the glaze has baked onto the loaf, 30 to 40 more minutes. An instant-read thermometer inserted into the thickest part of the loaf should read at least 160 degrees F (70 degrees C). Cooking time will depend on shape and thickness of the meatloaf.

GUMBO STYLE CHICKEN CREOLE

Servings: 6 | Prep: 15m | Cooks: 45m | Total: 1h

NUTRITION FACTS

Calories: 136.5 | Carbohydrates: 12.3g | Protein: 2.1g | Cholesterol: 0.5mg | Sodium: 735mg

INGREDIENTS

- 1/4 cup vegetable oil
- 1/4 cup all-purpose flour
- 1 green bell pepper, chopped
- 1 medium onion, chopped
- 2 cups cooked chicken, chopped
- 1 (14.5 ounce) can diced tomatoes with green chile peppers, with liquid
- 1 (4.5 ounce) can sliced mushrooms, drained
- 2 tablespoons chopped fresh parsley
- 2 teaspoons Worcestershire sauce
- 3 cloves garlic, minced
- 1 teaspoon soy sauce
- 1 teaspoon white sugar
- 1/2 teaspoon salt
- 1/2 teaspoon ground black pepper
- 3 dashes hot sauce, or to taste
- 1/2 cup chicken broth, or as needed

DIRECTIONS

1. Heat oil in a large skillet over high heat. Stir in flour and cook, stirring constantly, for 5 minutes or until mixture is the color of a copper penny. Reduce heat to low and stir in bell pepper and onion. Cook 10 to 15 minutes, or until tender, stirring occasionally.
2. Add chicken, tomatoes with green chile peppers, mushrooms, parsley, Worcestershire sauce, garlic, soy sauce, sugar, salt, pepper and hot sauce. Stir together, cover and simmer for 20 minutes. Add chicken broth or water if mixture is too thick for your liking.

MEATLESS MEATBALLS

Servings: 4 | Prep: 30m | Cooks: 1h | Total: 5h30m | Additional: 4h

NUTRITION FACTS

Calories: 421 | Carbohydrates: 50.1g | Fat: 17.9g | Protein: 16.9g | Cholesterol: 110mg

Sodium: 1695mg

INGREDIENTS

- 1 tablespoon olive oil
- 1 pound fresh white mushrooms, finely chopped
- 1 pinch salt
- 1 tablespoon butter
- 1/2 cup finely chopped onion
- 4 cloves garlic, minced
- 1/2 cup quick-cooking oats
- 1 ounce very finely shredded Parmigiano-Reggiano cheese
- 1/2 cup bread crumbs
- 1/4 cup chopped flat-leaf (Italian) parsley, packed
- 2 eggs, divided
- 1 teaspoon salt
- freshly ground black pepper to taste
- 1 pinch cayenne pepper, or to taste
- 1 pinch dried oregano
- 3 cups pasta sauce
- 1 tablespoon very finely shredded Parmigiano-Reggiano cheese, or to taste
- 1 tablespoon chopped flat-leaf (Italian) parsley, or to taste

DIRECTIONS

1. Heat olive oil in a skillet over medium-high heat. Add mushrooms to the hot oil, sprinkle with salt, and cook and stir until liquid from mushrooms has evaporated. Stir butter into mushrooms, reduce heat to medium, and cook and stir mushrooms until golden brown, about 5 minutes.
2. Stir onion into mushrooms and cook, stirring often, until onion is translucent, 5 minutes. Remove skillet from heat and stir garlic into mushroom mixture until fragrant, about 1 minute. Transfer mixture to a mixing bowl.
3. Mix oats into mushroom mixture until thoroughly combined. Gently stir 1 ounce Parmigiano-Reggiano cheese into mixture. Add bread crumbs, 1/4 cup parsley, and 1 egg; season with salt, black pepper, cayenne pepper, and oregano. Mix together with a fork until crumbly. Stir in remaining 1 egg. Mixture should hold together when pressed.

4. Cover bowl with plastic wrap and refrigerate at least 4 hours. For best flavor and texture, refrigerate overnight.

5. Preheat oven to 450 degrees F (230 degrees C). Line a baking sheet with a silicone baking mat or parchment paper.

6. Form mixture into small meatballs using a 2-tablespoon scoop. Roll meatballs lightly between your hands until smooth, if desired; arrange meatballs on prepared baking sheet.

7. Bake in the preheated oven until meatballs are lightly golden brown, 12 to 15 minutes.

8. Bring pasta sauce to a boil in a large saucepan; reduce heat to low. Gently stir meatballs into sauce until coated. Simmer meatballs in sauce until cooked through, 45 minutes to 1 hour. Transfer to a serving bowl and garnish with 1 tablespoon Parmigiano-Reggiano cheese and 1 tablespoon parsley.

MUSHROOM SLOW COOKER ROAST BEEF
Servings: 8 | Prep: 5m | Cooks: 9h | Total: 9h5m

NUTRITION FACTS

Calories: 388.4 | Carbohydrates: 6.2g | Protein: 24.4g | Cholesterol: 82.5mg | Sodium: 452.7mg

INGREDIENTS

- 1 pound sliced fresh mushrooms
- 1 (4 pound) standing beef rib roast
- 1 (1.25 ounce) envelope onion soup mix
- 1 (12 fluid ounce) bottle beer
- 1 pinch ground black pepper

DIRECTIONS

1. Place the mushrooms in the bottom of a slow cooker; set the roast atop the mushrooms; sprinkle the onion soup mix over the beef and pour the beer over everything; season with black pepper. Set slow cooker to LOW; cook 9 to 10 hours until the meat is easily pulled apart with a fork.

CHICKEN MARSALA FLORENTINE
Servings: 4 | Prep: 10m | Cooks: 25m | Total: 35m

NUTRITION FACTS

Calories: 670.9 | Carbohydrates: 24.6g | Protein: 32g | Cholesterol: 159.9mg | Sodium: 692.6mg

INGREDIENTS

- 4 boneless, skinless chicken breast halves
- 3/4 cup butter

- 1/4 cup all-purpose flour
- 1/4 teaspoon salt and pepper to taste
- 1 tablespoon dried oregano
- 2 tablespoons olive oil
- 3 cups sliced portobello mushrooms
- 3/4 cup sun-dried tomatoes
- 1/2 cup packed fresh spinach
- 1 cup Marsala wine

DIRECTIONS

1. Place chicken breasts between two pieces of wax paper, and pound to 1/4 inch thick with a meat mallet. Dust chicken with flour, salt , pepper and oregano.
2. In a skillet, fry chicken in olive oil over medium heat. Cook until done, turning to cook evenly. Set aside, and keep warm.
3. In the same pan, melt the butter over medium heat; add mushrooms, sun-dried tomatoes, and Marsala wine. Cook for approximately 10 minutes, stirring occasionally. Mix in spinach, and cook for about 2 minutes. Serve over chicken.

CREAMY MUSHROOM SOUP

Servings: 6 | Prep: 15m | Cooks: 1h20m | Total: 1h35m

NUTRITION FACTS

Calories: 272 | Carbohydrates: 12.2g | Fat: 23.3g | Protein: 6.9g | Cholesterol: 78mg | Sodium: 667mg

INGREDIENTS

- 1/4 cup unsalted butter
- 2 pounds sliced fresh mushrooms
- 1 pinch salt
- 1 yellow onion, diced
- 1 1/2 tablespoons all-purpose flour
- 6 sprigs fresh thyme
- 2 cloves garlic, peeled
- 4 cups chicken broth
- 1 cup water
- 1 cup heavy whipping cream
- 1 pinch salt and freshly ground black pepper to taste
- 1 teaspoon fresh thyme leaves for garnish, or to taste

DIRECTIONS

1. Melt butter in a large soup pot over medium-high heat; cook mushrooms in butter with 1 pinch salt until the mushrooms give off their juices; reduce heat to low. Continue to cook, stirring often, until juices evaporate and the mushrooms are golden brown, about 15 minutes. Set aside a few attractive mushroom slices for garnish later, if desired. Mix onion into mushrooms and cook until onion is soft and translucent, about 5 more minutes.
2. Stir flour into mushroom mixture and cook, stirring often, for 2 minutes to remove raw flour taste. Tie thyme sprigs into a small bundle with kitchen twine and add to mushroom mixture; add garlic cloves. Pour chicken stock and water into mushroom mixture. Bring to a simmer and cook for 1 hour. Remove thyme bundle.
3. Transfer soup to a blender in small batches and puree on high speed until smooth and thick.
4. Return soup to pot and stir in cream. Season with salt and black pepper and serve in bowls, garnished with reserved mushroom slices and a few thyme leaves.

PORK CHOP AND POTATO CASSEROLE

Servings: 5 | Prep: 20m | Cooks: 1h | Total: 1h20m

NUTRITION FACTS

Calories: 705.4 | Carbohydrates: 37.9g | Protein: 32.7g | Cholesterol: 122.7mg | Sodium: 635.9mg

INGREDIENTS

- 1 tablespoon vegetable oil
- 6 boneless pork chops
- 1 (10.75 ounce) can condensed cream of mushroom soup
- 1 cup milk
- 4 medium (2-1/4" to 3" dia, raw)s potatoes, thinly sliced
- 1/2 cup chopped onion
- 1 cup shredded Cheddar cheese

DIRECTIONS

1. Preheat oven to 400 degrees F (200 degrees C).
2. Heat oil in a large skillet over medium high-heat. Place the pork chops in the oil, and sear.
3. In a medium bowl, combine the soup and the milk. Arrange the potatoes and onions in a 9x13 inch baking dish. Place the browned chops over the potatoes and onions, then pour the soup mixture over all.
4. Bake 30 minutes in the preheated oven. Top with the cheese, and bake for 30 more minutes.

BUSY DAY CHICKEN RICE CASSEROLE

Servings: 8 | Prep: 10m | Cooks: 2h | Total: 2h10m

NUTRITION FACTS

Calories: 291.1 | Carbohydrates: 27.7g | Protein: 30.5g | Cholesterol: 72.6mg | Sodium: 988mg

INGREDIENTS

- 1 (10.75 ounce) can condensed cream of mushroom soup
- 1 (10.75 ounce) can condensed cream of celery soup
- 1 cup water
- 1 cup uncooked white rice
- 1 (4.5 ounce) can mushrooms, drained
- 1 pinch garlic powder
- ground black pepper to taste
- 1 (1 ounce) package dry onion soup mix
- 8 skinless, boneless chicken breast halves

DIRECTIONS

1. Preheat oven to 325 degrees F (165 degrees C).
2. In a large bowl combine the mushroom soup, celery soup, water, rice, mushrooms, garlic powder and black pepper. Mix all together. Pour mixture into a 9x13 inch baking dish and spread on bottom.
3. Lay chicken pieces over soup mixture and sprinkle dry onion soup mix over all. Cover tightly with aluminum foil and bake in the preheated oven for 1 to 1 1/2 hours or until chicken is cooked through and no longer pink inside.

EASY TURKEY TETRAZZINI

Servings: 6 | Prep: 20m | Cooks: 25m | Total: 45m

NUTRITION FACTS

Calories: 411.1 | Carbohydrates: 33.5g | Protein: 24g | Cholesterol: 105.3mg | Sodium: 1081.1mg

INGREDIENTS

- 1 (8 ounce) package cooked egg noodles
- 2 tablespoons butter
- 2 cups chopped cooked turkey
- 1 (10.75 ounce) can condensed cream of celery soup

- 1 (6 ounce) can sliced mushrooms
- 1 teaspoon salt
- 1/8 teaspoon pepper
- 1 cup sour cream
- 1/2 cup grated Parmesan cheese

DIRECTIONS

1. Bring a large pot of lightly salted water to a boil. Add pasta and cook for 8 to 10 minutes or until al dente; drain. Preheat oven to 375 degrees F (190 degrees C).
2. Melt butter in a large heavy skillet. Saute mushrooms for 1 minute. Season with salt and pepper, and stir in turkey, condensed soup, and sour cream. Place cooked noodles in a 9x13 inch baking dish. Pour sauce mixture evenly over the top. Sprinkle with Parmesan cheese.
3. Bake in preheated oven for 20 to 25 minutes, or until sauce is bubbling.

GRILLED PORTOBELLO MUSHROOMS

Servings: 3 | Prep: 10m | Cooks: 10m | Total: 1h20m | Additional: 1h

NUTRITION FACTS

Calories: 217.1 | Carbohydrates: 11g | Protein: 3.2g | Cholesterol: 0mg | Sodium: 12.9mg

INGREDIENTS

- 3 portobello mushrooms
- 1/4 cup canola oil
- 3 tablespoons chopped onion
- 4 cloves garlic, minced
- 4 tablespoons balsamic vinegar

DIRECTIONS

1. Clean mushrooms and remove stems, reserve for other use. Place caps on a plate with the gills up.
2. In a small bowl, combine the oil, onion, garlic and vinegar. Pour mixture evenly over the mushroom caps and let stand for 1 hour.
3. Grill over hot grill for 10 minutes. Serve immediately.

CHICAGO-STYLE PAN PIZZA

Servings: 6 | Prep: 30m | Cooks: 35m | Total: 1h5m

NUTRITION FACTS

Calories: 578 | Carbohydrates: 46.8g | Fat: 27.4g | Protein: 32.3g | Cholesterol: 61mg | Sodium: 1816mg

INGREDIENTS

- 1 (1 pound) loaf frozen bread dough, thawed
- 1 pound bulk Italian sausage
- 2 cups shredded mozzarella cheese
- 8 ounces sliced fresh mushrooms
- 1 small onion, chopped
- 2 teaspoons olive oil
- 1 (28 ounce) can diced tomatoes, drained
- 3/4 teaspoon dried oregano
- 1/2 teaspoon salt
- 1/4 teaspoon fennel seed
- 1/4 teaspoon garlic powder
- 1/2 cup freshly grated Parmesan cheese

DIRECTIONS

1. Preheat the oven to 350 degrees F (175 degrees C). Press the dough into the bottom and up the sides of a greased 9x13 inch baking dish.
2. Crumble the sausage into a large skillet over medium-high heat. Cook and stir until evenly browned. Remove the sausage with a slotted spoon, and sprinkle over the dough crust. Sprinkle mozzarella cheese evenly over the sausage.
3. Add mushrooms and onion to the skillet; cook and stir until the onion is tender. Stir in the tomatoes, oregano, salt, fennel seed and garlic powder. Spoon over the mozzarella cheese. Sprinkle Parmesan cheese over the top.
4. Bake for 25 to 35 minutes in the preheated oven, or until crust is golden brown.

CHICKEN LO MEIN

Servings: 4 | Prep: 45m | Cooks: 30m | Total: 2h15m | Additional: 1h

NUTRITION FACTS

Calories: 598.6 | Carbohydrates: 78.6g | Protein: 38g | Cholesterol: 60.8mg | Sodium: 1877mg

INGREDIENTS

- 4 skinless, boneless chicken breast halves -
- 2 tablespoons cornstarch

cut into thin strips

- 5 teaspoons white sugar, divided
- 3 tablespoons rice wine vinegar
- 1/2 cup soy sauce, divided
- 1 1/4 cups chicken broth
- 1 cup water
- 1 tablespoon sesame oil
- 1/2teaspoon ground black pepper
- 1 (12 ounce) package uncooked linguine pasta
- 2 tablespoons vegetable oil, divided
- 2 tablespoons minced fresh ginger root
- 1 tablespoon minced garlic
- 1/2pound fresh shiitake mushrooms, stemmed and sliced
- 6 green onions, sliced diagonally into 1/2 inch pieces

DIRECTIONS

1. In a medium, non-reactive bowl, combine the chicken with 2 1/2 teaspoons of white sugar, 1 1/2 tablespoons vinegar and 1/4 cup soy sauce. Mix this together and coat the chicken well. Cover and let marinate in the refrigerator for at least 1 hour.
2. In another medium bowl, combine the chicken broth, water, sesame oil and ground black pepper with the remaining sugar, vinegar and soy sauce. In a separate small bowl, dissolve the cornstarch with some of this mixture and slowly add to the bulk of the mixture, stirring well. Set aside.
3. Cook the linguine according to package directions, drain and set aside. Heat 1 tablespoon of the vegetable oil in a wok or large saucepan over high heat until it starts to smoke. Add the chicken and stir-fry for 4 to 5 minutes, or until browned. Transfer this and all juices to a warm plate.
4. Heat the remaining vegetable oil in the wok or pan over high heat. Add the ginger, garlic, mushrooms and green onions, and stir-fry for 30 seconds. Add the reserved sauce mixture and then the chicken. Simmer until the sauce begins to thicken, about 2 minutes. Add the reserved noodles and toss gently, coating everything well with the sauce.

PORK CHOPS IN GARLIC MUSHROOM SAUCE

Servings: 8 | Prep: 10m | Cooks: 20m | Total: 30m

NUTRITION FACTS

Calories: 198.9 | Carbohydrates: 3.1g | Protein: 16.3g | Cholesterol: 53.9mg | Sodium: 332.7mg

INGREDIENTS

- 2 pounds boneless pork chops
- 1/2 teaspoon paprika
- 1 pinch kosher salt and ground black pepper to taste
- 1/4 cup butter, divided
- 1 (8 ounce) package sliced fresh mushrooms
- 4 cloves garlic, minced
- 1 teaspoon Dijon mustard
- 2 tablespoons all-purpose flour
- 2 cups beef broth

DIRECTIONS

1. Season both sides of pork chops with paprika, salt, and pepper.
2. Heat a large skillet over medium-high heat; add 2 tablespoons butter. Sear pork chops until golden brown and no longer pink in the center, 2 to 4 minutes per side. Remove pork chops from the skillet and set aside.
3. Melt remaining butter in the same skillet over medium-high heat. Add mushrooms and cook until golden and excess moisture evaporates, about 5 minutes. Add garlic and mustard; cook until garlic is fragrant, about 1 minute.
4. Add flour to the skillet, stirring to remove any lumps. Slowly add beef broth, whisking until incorporated. Season with salt and pepper. Reduce heat to medium and simmer, stirring often, until sauce thickens, about 5 minutes. Check for seasoning again.
5. Return pork chops to the skillet and cook until heated through, about 1 minute. Serve hot.

BACON AND CHEDDAR STUFFED MUSHROOMS

Servings: 8 | Prep: 15m | Cooks: 15m | Total: 30m

NUTRITION FACTS

Calories: 110 | Carbohydrates: 0.9g | Protein: 4.7g | Cholesterol: 22.1mg | Sodium: 170.5mg

INGREDIENTS

- 3 slices bacon
- 8 crimini mushrooms
- 1 tablespoon butter
- 1 tablespoon chopped onion
- 3/4 cup shredded Cheddar cheese

DIRECTIONS

1. Place bacon in a large, deep skillet. Cook over medium high heat until evenly brown. Drain, dice and set aside.
2. Preheat oven to 400 degrees F (200 degrees C).
3. Remove mushroom stems. Set aside caps. Chop the stems.
4. In a large saucepan over medium heat, melt the butter. Slowly cook and stir the chopped stems and onion until the onion is soft. Remove from heat.
5. In a medium bowl, stir together the mushroom stem mixture, bacon and 1/2 cup Cheddar. Mix well and scoop the mixture into the mushroom caps.
6. Bake in the preheated oven 15 minutes, or until the cheese has melted.
7. Remove the mushrooms from the oven, and sprinkle with the remaining cheese.

MUSHROOM ORZO

Servings: 6 | Prep: 15m | Cooks: 25m | Total: 40m

NUTRITION FACTS

Calories: 327.4 | Carbohydrates: 28.1g | Protein: 8.6g | Cholesterol: 48mg | Sodium: 241.3mg

INGREDIENTS

- 1/2 cup butter, divided
- 8 eaches pearl onions
- 1 cup uncooked orzo pasta
- 1/2 cup sliced fresh mushrooms
- 1 cup water
- 1/2 cup white wine
- 1 pinch garlic powder to taste
- 1 pinch salt and pepper to taste
- 1/2 cup grated Parmesan cheese
- 1/4 cup fresh parsley

DIRECTIONS

1. Melt 1/2 the butter in a skillet over medium heat. Stir in the onions, and cook until golden brown. Mix in orzo, mushrooms, and remaining butter. Cook and stir 5 minutes, until butter is melted and mushrooms are tender.
2. Pour water and wine into the skillet, and bring to a boil. Reduce heat to low. Season with garlic powder, salt, and pepper. Cook 7 to 10 minutes, until orzo is al dente. Stir in the Parmesan cheese and parsley to serve.

SAVORY CRAB STUFFED MUSHROOMS

Servings: 8 | Prep: 25m | Cooks: 20m | Total: 45m

NUTRITION FACTS

Calories: 176.4 | Carbohydrates: 7.3g | Protein: 9.8g | Cholesterol: 64.6mg | Sodium: 233.3mg

INGREDIENTS

- 3 tablespoons butter, melted
- 24 fresh mushrooms
- 2 tablespoons butter
- 2 tablespoons minced green onions
- 1 teaspoon lemon juice
- 1 cup diced cooked crabmeat
- 1/2 cup soft bread crumbs
- 1 egg, beaten
- 1/2 teaspoon dried dill weed
- 3/4 cup shredded Monterey Jack cheese, divided
- 1/4 cup dry white wine

DIRECTIONS

1. Preheat oven to 400 degrees F (200 degrees C). Prepare a 9x13 inch baking dish with 3 tablespoons butter.
2. Remove stems from mushrooms. Set aside caps. Finely chop stems.
3. Melt 2 tablespoons butter in a medium saucepan over medium heat. Stir in the chopped stems and green onions and cook until soft, about 3 minutes. Remove saucepan from heat. Stir in lemon juice, crabmeat, soft bread crumbs, egg, dill weed and 1/4 cup Monterey Jack cheese. Thoroughly blend the mixture.
4. Place mushroom caps in the buttered pan, and stir until caps are coated with the butter. Arrange caps cavity side up, and stuff cavities generously with the green onion and crabmeat mixture. Top with remaining Monterey Jack cheese. Pour wine into the pan around the mushrooms.
5. Bake uncovered in the preheated oven 15 to 20 minutes, until cheese is melted and lightly browned. Serve warm.

CHICKEN BREASTS STUFFED WITH PERFECTION

Servings: 6 | Prep: 1h | Cooks: 45m | Total: 2h45m | Additional: 1h

NUTRITION FACTS

Calories: 622.4 | Carbohydrates: 34.7g | Protein: 43.4g | Cholesterol: 119mg | Sodium: 1516.6mg

INGREDIENTS

- 6 skinless, boneless chicken breast halves - pounded thin
- 1 (8 ounce) bottle Italian-style salad dressing
- 8 slices of stale wheat bread, torn
- 3/4 cup grated Parmesan cheese
- 1 teaspoon chopped fresh thyme
- 1/8 teaspoon pepper
- 1 1/2 cups feta cheese, crumbled
- 1/2 cup sour cream
- 1 tablespoon vegetable oil
- 3 cloves garlic, minced
- 4 cups chopped fresh spinach
- 1 bunch green onions, chopped
- 1 cup mushrooms, sliced
- 1 (8 ounce) jar oil-packed sun-dried tomatoes, chopped

DIRECTIONS

1. Place chicken breasts in a large resealable plastic bag. Pour in Italian dressing, seal tightly, and refrigerate at least 1 hour.
2. Place the stale bread, Parmesan, thyme, and pepper into a food processor. Pulse until the bread is processed into crumbs. Seat aside.
3. In a large bowl, stir together the feta and sour cream. Set aside.
4. Heat the oil in a large skillet over medium heat. Stir in the garlic. Then add the spinach, and cook until it wilts. Stir in green onions, cook 2 minutes. Remove spinach to a plate, and leave any liquid in the pan. Stir in mushrooms, and saute until soft. Remove mushrooms to plate with spinach. Allow to cool briefly, then combine spinach and mushrooms with feta and sour cream mixture.
5. Stir the sun-dried tomatoes into the mixture, and spread onto a large cookie sheet. Place in the freezer for about 30 minutes.
6. Preheat the oven to 400 degrees F (200 degrees C).
7. Place chicken breasts on a cookie sheet, and place about 3 tablespoons of the filling mixture in the center of each breast. Roll the breasts, and secure with a toothpick. Transfer chicken breasts to a baking dish, and sprinkle breadcrumb mixture over chicken breasts.
8. Bake, uncovered, in a preheated oven for 25 minutes.

THAI CHICKEN WITH BASIL STIR FRY

Servings: 6 | Prep: 15m | Cooks: 20m | Total: 35m

NUTRITION FACTS

Calories: 505.5 | Carbohydrates: 60g | Protein: 36.9g | Cholesterol: 78mg | Sodium: 804.4mg

INGREDIENTS

- 2 cups uncooked jasmine rice
- 1 quart water
- 3/4 cup coconut milk
- 3 tablespoons soy sauce
- 3 tablespoons rice wine vinegar
- 1 1/2 tablespoons fish sauce
- 3/4 teaspoon red pepper flakes
- 1 tablespoon olive oil

- 1 medium onion, sliced
- 2 tablespoons fresh ginger root, minced
- 3 cloves garlic, minced
- 2 pounds skinless, boneless chicken breast halves - cut into 1/2 inch strips
- 3 shiitake mushrooms, sliced
- 5 green onions, chopped
- 1 1/2 cups chopped fresh basil leaves

DIRECTIONS

1. Bring rice and water to a boil in a pot. Cover, reduce heat to low, and simmer 20 minutes.
2. In a bowl, mix the coconut milk, soy sauce, rice wine vinegar, fish sauce, and red pepper flakes.
3. In a skillet or wok, heat the oil over medium-high heat. Stir in the onion, ginger, and garlic, and cook until lightly browned. Mix in chicken strips, and cook about 3 minutes, until browned. Stir in the coconut milk sauce. Continue cooking until sauce is reduced be about 1/3. Mix in mushrooms, green onions, and basil, and cook until heated through. Serve over the cooked rice.

BACON MUSHROOM CHICKEN

Servings: 2 | Prep: 15m | Cooks: 1h | Total: 1h15m

NUTRITION FACTS

Calories: 773.9 | Carbohydrates: 2.7g | Protein: 52.7g | Cholesterol: 241.1mg | Sodium: 1011.3mg

INGREDIENTS

- 2 tablespoons butter, melted
- 2 bone-in chicken breast halves, with skin
- 1 teaspoon seasoning salt

- 2 thick slices bacon
- 1/2 cup mushrooms, halved
- 1/4 cup heavy cream

* 1 clove garlic, crushed

DIRECTIONS

1. Preheat oven to 350 degrees F (175 degrees C).
2. Pour melted butter into a 9x13 inch baking dish. Add chicken, skin side down; sprinkle with seasoning salt and garlic. Turn chicken over, season, and lay bacon strips on top. Sprinkle with mushrooms.
3. Bake in preheated oven for 45 minutes to 60 minutes, or until chicken is no longer pink and juices run clear.
4. Remove chicken, bacon and mushrooms to a platter and keep warm. Pour juices from baking dish into a small saucepan and whisk together with cream over low heat until thickened. Pour sauce over chicken and serve warm.

CHICKEN AND SPINACH ALFREDO LASAGNA

Servings: 12 | Prep: 30m | Cooks: 1h30m | Total: 2h

NUTRITION FACTS

Calories: 591.3 | Carbohydrates: 22g | Protein: 28.7g | Cholesterol: 159.5mg | Sodium: 846.8mg

INGREDIENTS

* 1 (8 ounce) package lasagna noodles
* 3 cups heavy cream
* 2 (10.75 ounce) cans condensed cream of mushroom soup
* 1 cup grated Parmesan cheese
* 1/4 cup butter
* 1 tablespoon olive oil
* 1/2 large onion, diced
* 4 cloves garlic, sliced
* 5 mushrooms, diced
* 1 roasted chicken, shredded
* 1/2 teaspoon salt and ground black pepper to taste
* 1 cup ricotta cheese
* 1 bunch fresh spinach, rinsed
* 3 cups shredded mozzarella cheese

DIRECTIONS

1. Preheat oven to 350 degrees F (175 degrees C). Bring a large pot of lightly salted water to a boil. Cook lasagna noodles for 8 to 10 minutes, or until al dente. Drain, and rinse with cold water.

2. In a saucepan over low heat, mix together heavy cream, cream of mushroom soup, Parmesan cheese, and butter. Simmer, stirring frequently, until well blended.
3. Heat the olive oil in a skillet over medium heat. Cook and stir the onion in olive oil until tender, then add garlic and mushrooms. Mix in the chicken, and cook until heated through. Season with salt and pepper.
4. Lightly coat the bottom of a 9x13 inch baking dish with enough of the cream sauce mixture to coat. Layer with 1/3 of the lasagna noodles, 1/2 cup ricotta, 1/2 of the spinach, 1/2 the chicken mixture, and 1 cup mozzarella. Top with 1/3 the cream sauce mixture, and repeat the layers. Place the remaining noodles on top, and spread with remaining sauce.
5. Bake 1 hour in the preheated oven, or until brown and bubbly. Top with the remaining mozzarella, and continue baking until cheese is melted and lightly browned.

ROASTED ASPARAGUS AND MUSHROOMS

Servings: 6 | Prep: 10m | Cooks: 15m | Total: 25m

NUTRITION FACTS

Calories: 37.9 | Carbohydrates: 4.3g | Protein: 2.8g | Cholesterol: 0mg | Sodium: 83.5mg

INGREDIENTS

- 1 bunch fresh asparagus, trimmed
- 1/2 pound fresh mushrooms, quartered
- 2 sprigs fresh rosemary, minced
- 2 teaspoons olive oil
- 1/4 teaspoon kosher salt to taste
- 1/8 teaspoon freshly ground black pepper to taste

DIRECTIONS

1. Preheat oven to 450 degrees F (230 degrees C). Lightly spray a cookie sheet with vegetable cooking spray.
2. Place the asparagus and mushrooms in a bowl. Drizzle with the olive oil, then season with rosemary, salt, and pepper; toss well. Lay the asparagus and mushrooms out on the prepared pan in an even layer. Roast in the preheated oven until the asparagus is tender, about 15 minutes.

LEMON MUSHROOM HERB CHICKEN

Servings: 4 | Prep: 15m | Cooks: 30m | Total: 45m

NUTRITION FACTS

Calories: 567.9 | Carbohydrates: 36.2g | Protein: 36.4g | Cholesterol: 130.2mg | Sodium: 1914.7mg

INGREDIENTS

- 1 cup all-purpose flour
- 1/2 tablespoon dried thyme
- 2 tablespoons dried basil
- 1 tablespoon dried parsley
- 1 teaspoon paprika
- 1 teaspoon salt
- 1/2 teaspoon ground black pepper
- 1 teaspoon garlic powder
- 4 boneless, skinless chicken breast halves
- 1/2 cup butter
- 1 (10.75 ounce) can condensed cream of mushroom soup
- 1 (10.5 ounce) can condensed chicken broth
- 1/4 cup dry white wine
- 1 lemon, juiced
- 1 tablespoon chopped fresh parsley
- 2 tablespoons capers
- 1 tablespoon grated lemon zest

DIRECTIONS

1. In a shallow dish or bowl, combine the flour, thyme, basil, parsley, paprika, salt, ground black pepper, and garlic powder. Dredge chicken in the mixture to coat, patting off any excess flour.
2. Melt butter in a large skillet over medium heat, and cook chicken until no longer translucent. In a medium bowl, mix together the cream of mushroom soup, chicken broth, wine, and lemon juice; pour over chicken.
3. Cover skillet, and simmer 20 minutes, or until chicken is no longer pink and juices run clear. Garnish with parsley, capers, and lemon zest.

MUSHROOM RISOTTO

Servings: 4 | Prep: 10m | Cooks: 35m | Total: 45m

NUTRITION FACTS

Calories: 438.8 | Carbohydrates: 48.7g | Protein: 16.9g | Cholesterol: 49.9mg | Sodium: 767.6mg

INGREDIENTS

- 1 tablespoon olive oil
- 3 small onions, finely chopped
- 1 cup whole milk
- 1/4 cup heavy cream

- 1 clove garlic, crushed
- 1 teaspoon minced fresh parsley
- 1 teaspoon minced celery
- salt and pepper to taste
- 1 1/2 cups sliced fresh mushrooms
- 1 cup rice
- 5 cups vegetable stock
- 1 teaspoon butter
- 1 cup grated Parmesan cheese

DIRECTIONS

1. Heat olive oil in a large skillet over medium-high heat. Saute the onion and garlic in the olive oil until onion is tender and garlic is lightly browned. Remove garlic, and stir in the parsley, celery, salt, and pepper. Cook until celery is tender, then add the mushrooms. Reduce heat to low, and continue cooking until the mushrooms are soft.
2. Pour the milk and cream into the skillet, and stir in the rice. Heat to a simmer. Stir the vegetable stock into the rice one cup at a time, until it is absorbed.
3. When the rice has finished cooking, stir in the butter and Parmesan cheese, and remove from heat. Serve hot.

PAPRIKA CHICKEN WITH MUSHROOMS

Servings: 4 | Prep: 15m | Cooks: 25m | Total: 40m

NUTRITION FACTS

Calories: 259.5 | Carbohydrates: 6.8g | Protein: 27g | Cholesterol: 91.3mg | Sodium: 138.5mg

INGREDIENTS

- 4 skinless, boneless chicken breasts
- 1 teaspoon paprika
- 1 pinch salt and pepper to taste
- 1 pinch garlic powder
- 1/4 cup butter
- 1 onion, sliced into thin rings
- 1 pound fresh mushrooms, sliced

DIRECTIONS

1. Pound chicken breasts to 1/2 inch thickness. Sprinkle both sides of each chicken breast liberally with paprika, salt, pepper, and garlic powder.

2. In a large skillet, melt the butter over medium heat. Arrange chicken breasts in the pan, cover, and cook for 10 minutes. Turn chicken breasts over, and layer the thinly sliced onions and mushrooms on top of the chicken. Cover, and cook for 10 minutes.

3. Remove lid, and mix onions and mushrooms into the butter sauce. Reduce heat to low, and cook uncovered for 5 minutes.

DINAH'S STUFFED MUSHROOMS

Servings: 10 | Prep: 20m | Cooks: 30m | Total: 50m

NUTRITION FACTS

Calories: 383.3 | Carbohydrates: 11.2g | Protein: 15.5g | Cholesterol: 106mg | Sodium: 412mg

INGREDIENTS

- 20 fresh mushrooms, stems removed
- 2 (6.5 ounce) cans minced clams, drained
- 2 cloves garlic, peeled and minced
- 1/2 cup grated Parmesan cheese
- 1 small onion, finely chopped
- 3/4 cup dry bread crumbs
- 1/2 cup chopped green bell pepper
- 2 tablespoons dried parsley
- 2 tablespoons Italian-style seasoning
- ground black pepper to taste
- 1 1/2 cups butter, melted
- 1/2 cup shredded mozzarella cheese

DIRECTIONS

1. Preheat oven to 350 degrees F (175 degrees C). Lightly grease a 9x13 inch baking dish.
2. Arrange mushroom caps hollow side up in the baking dish.
3. In a medium bowl, mix together minced clams, garlic, Parmesan cheese, onion, bread crumbs, green bell pepper, parsley, Italian-style seasoning and black pepper. Slowly stir in approximately 1/2 the butter, enough to make the mixture slightly moist.
4. Generously fill the mushroom caps with the clam mixture. Sprinkle with mozzarella cheese. Drizzle with remaining butter.
5. Bake in the preheated oven 30 minutes, or until lightly browned.

PAT'S MUSHROOM SAUTE

Servings: 4 | Prep: 5m | Cooks: 30m | Total: 35m

NUTRITION FACTS

Calories: 93.8 | Carbohydrates: 5.3g | Protein: 2.3g | Cholesterol: 15.3mg | Sodium: 45.6mg

INGREDIENTS

- 2 tablespoons butter
- 1/2 tablespoon olive oil
- 1/2 tablespoon balsamic vinegar
- 1 clove garlic, minced
- 1/8 teaspoon dried oregano
- 1 pound button mushrooms, sliced

DIRECTIONS

1. Melt butter with oil in a large skillet over medium heat. Stir in balsamic vinegar, garlic, oregano, and mushrooms. Saute for 20 to 30 minutes, or until tender.

SANDY'S CASSEROLE

Servings: 6 | Prep: 5m | Cooks: 45m | Total: 50m

NUTRITION FACTS

Calories: 508 | Carbohydrates: 40.2g | Protein: 30.3g | Cholesterol: 83.5mg | Sodium: 1252.8mg

INGREDIENTS

- 2 cups uncooked elbow macaroni
- 2 (5 ounce) cans chunk chicken
- 2 cups shredded Cheddar cheese
- 2 cups milk
- 2 (10.75 ounce) cans condensed cream of chicken soup
- 1 (4 ounce) can sliced mushrooms
- 1/4 cup chopped onion

DIRECTIONS

1. Preheat oven to 350 degrees F (175 degrees C).
2. In a large bowl combine the macaroni, chicken, cheese, milk, soup, mushrooms and onion. Mix together and transfer mixture to a 9x13 inch baking dish.

3. Bake at 350 degrees F (175 degrees C) for about 45 minutes, or until bubbly and golden brown.

POTATO CASSEROLE

Servings: 12 | Prep: 15m | Cooks: 1h10m | Total: 1h25m

NUTRITION FACTS

Calories: 400 | Carbohydrates: 23.1g | Protein: 8.5g | Cholesterol: 77.1mg | Sodium: 483.4mg

INGREDIENTS

- 1 (30 ounce) package frozen hash brown potatoes
- 2 cups shredded Cheddar cheese
- 1 (16 ounce) container sour cream
- 1 (10.75 ounce) can condensed cream of mushroom soup
- 1 onion, chopped
- 1 cup butter
- 3 cups crushed corn flakes

DIRECTIONS

1. Preheat oven to 425 degrees F (220 degrees C).
2. Pour the hash browns into a lightly greased 9x13 inch baking dish. In a large bowl, combine the cheese, sour cream and soup.
3. In a large skillet over medium heat, combine the onion with 1 stick butter and saute for 5 minutes. Add this to the soup mixture and spread this over the potatoes in the dish.
4. Next, arrange the crushed corn flakes over all in the dish. Melt the remaining stick of butter and pour this evenly over the corn flakes.
5. Bake at 425 degrees F (220 degrees C) for 1 hour.

GRILLED STUFFED PORTOBELLO MUSHROOMS

Servings: 4 | Prep: 15m | Cooks: 20m | Total: 35m

NUTRITION FACTS

Calories: 156.5 | Carbohydrates: 7.3g | Protein: 3.1g | Cholesterol: 0mg | Sodium: 589.4mg

INGREDIENTS

- 1/2 cup finely chopped red bell pepper
- 1 teaspoon salt

- 1 clove garlic, minced
- 1/4 cup olive oil
- 1/4 teaspoon onion powder
- 1/2 teaspoon ground black pepper
- 4 portobello mushroom caps

DIRECTIONS

1. Preheat grill for medium heat.
2. In a large bowl, mix the red bell pepper, garlic, oil, onion powder, salt, and ground black pepper. Spread mixture over gill side of the mushroom caps.
3. Lightly oil the grill grate. Place mushrooms over indirect heat, cover, and cook for 15 to 20 minutes.

CHICKEN OR TURKEY TETRAZZINI DELUXE

Servings: 12 | Prep: 25m | Cooks: 35m | Total: 1h

NUTRITION FACTS

Calories: 493.4 | Carbohydrates: 39g | Protein: 28.8g | Cholesterol: 85.3mg | Sodium: 943.9mg

INGREDIENTS

- 1 (16 ounce) package linguine pasta
- 1/2 cup butter
- 3 cups sliced fresh mushrooms
- 1 cup minced onion
- 1 cup minced green bell pepper
- 2 (10.75 ounce) cans condensed cream of mushroom soup
- 2 cups chicken broth
- 2 cups shredded sharp Cheddar cheese
- 1 (10 ounce) package frozen green peas
- 1/2 cup cooking sherry
- 1 teaspoon Worcestershire sauce
- 1 teaspoon salt
- 1/4 teaspoon ground black pepper
- 4 cups chopped cooked chicken breast
- 1 cup grated Parmesan cheese
- paprika to taste

DIRECTIONS

1. Bring a large pot of lightly salted water to a boil. Add pasta and cook for 8 to 10 minutes or until al dente; drain and set aside.

2. Preheat oven to 375 degrees F (190 degrees C).

3. Meanwhile, melt butter in a large saucepan over medium heat. Add mushrooms, onion and bell pepper and saute until tender. Stir in cream of mushroom soup and chicken broth; cook, stirring, until heated through. Stir in pasta, Cheddar cheese, peas, sherry, Worcestershire sauce, salt, pepper and chicken. Mix well and transfer mixture to a lightly greased 11x14 inch baking dish. Sprinkle with Parmesan cheese and paprika.

4. Bake in the preheated oven for 25 to 35 minutes, or until heated through.

SLOW COOKER CHICKEN WITH MUSHROOM WINE SAUCE

Servings: 4 | Prep: 10m | Cooks: 6h | Total: 6h10m

NUTRITION FACTS

Calories: 207.8 | Carbohydrates: 7.6g | Protein: 24.9g | Cholesterol: 61.1mg | Sodium: 955.9mg

INGREDIENTS

- 1 (10.75 ounce) can condensed cream of mushroom soup
- 1 teaspoon dried minced onion
- 1 teaspoon dried parsley
- 1/4 cup white wine
- 1/4 teaspoon garlic powder
- 1 tablespoon milk
- 1 (4 ounce) can mushroom pieces, drained
- 1/2 teaspoon salt and pepper to taste
- 4 boneless, skinless chicken breast halves

DIRECTIONS

1. In a slow cooker, mix together the soup, onion, parsley, wine, garlic powder, milk, and mushroom pieces. Season with salt and pepper. Place chicken in the slow cooker, covering with the soup mixture.

2. Cook on Low setting for 5 to 6 hours, or on High setting for 3 to 4 hours.

CHICKEN, ASPARAGUS, AND MUSHROOM SKILLET

Servings: 2 | Prep: 15m | Cooks: 25m | Total: 40m

NUTRITION FACTS

Calories: 429.9 | Carbohydrates: 7.3g | Protein: 26.9g | Cholesterol: 106.6mg | Sodium: 491mg

INGREDIENTS

- 3 tablespoons butter
- 2 tablespoons olive oil
- 1/2 teaspoon dried parsley
- 1/2 teaspoon dried basil
- 1/8 teaspoon dried oregano
- 1 1/2 cloves garlic, minced
- 1/4 teaspoon salt
- 1 1/2 teaspoons lemon juice
- 1 1/2 teaspoons white cooking wine
- 2 skinless, boneless chicken breast halves, sliced
- 1/2 pound fresh asparagus, trimmed and cut into thirds
- 1 cup sliced fresh mushrooms

DIRECTIONS

1. Melt the butter with the olive oil in a skillet over medium-high; stir the parsley, basil, oregano, garlic, salt, lemon juice, and wine into the butter mixture. Add the chicken; cook and stir until the chicken is browned, about 3 minutes. Reduce heat to medium; cook, stirring occasionally, until the chicken is no longer pink inside, about 10 more minutes.
2. Add the asparagus; cook and stir until the asparagus is bright green and just starting to become tender, about 3 minutes. Stir in the mushrooms and cook an additional 3 minutes to let the mushrooms release their juice. Serve hot.

MUSHROOM GRAVY

Servings: 6 | Prep: 10m | Cooks: 50m | Total: 1h

NUTRITION FACTS

Calories: 133 | Carbohydrates: 8.9g | Fat: 8.7g | Protein: 5.7g | Cholesterol: 20mg | Sodium: 63mg

INGREDIENTS

- 1/4 cup butter
- 1 quart beef stock

* 1 (16 ounce) package
  sliced mushrooms
* salt to taste
* 1/4 cup all-purpose flour,
  or as needed

* 1 pinch ground black
  pepper to taste
* fresh thyme leaves, to
  taste (optional)

DIRECTIONS

1. Heat butter over medium heat in a saucepan until it foams. Stir in mushrooms. Season with salt.
   Simmer until liquid evaporates, about 20 minutes.
2. Stir in the flour, cooking and stirring for about 5 minutes. Add about 1 cup of beef stock, stirring
   briskly until incorporated, then pour in the remaining stock and mix thoroughly. Season with black
   pepper and thyme. Reduce heat to medium-low, and simmer until thickened, about 30 minutes,
   stirring often.

SKILLET CHOPS WITH MUSHROOM GRAVY

Servings: 4 | Prep: 10m | Cooks: 30m | Total: 40m

NUTRITION FACTS

Calories: 318.7 | Carbohydrates: 16.4g | Protein: 28.1g | Cholesterol: 64mg | Sodium: 705mg

INGREDIENTS

* 1/2 cup dry bread crumbs
* 2 tablespoons grated
  Parmesan cheese
* 4 pork chops

* 1 tablespoon vegetable oil
* 1 (10.75 ounce) can
  condensed cream of
  mushroom soup
* 1/2 cup milk

DIRECTIONS

1. Combine bread crumbs and Parmesan cheese in a large resealable plastic bag. Add chops two at a
   time, and shake to coat.
2. Heat oil in a large skillet over medium-high heat, and cook chops until brown on both sides. Remove
   chops from skillet, and reduce heat to medium.
3. Blend soup and milk in the skillet, stirring to scrape up the bits of breading left over from the chops.
   You can adjust the amount of milk depending on how thick you want the gravy to be (it will thin a
   bit during the cooking process). Bring to a gentle boil, increasing heat slightly if necessary. When
   soup mixture is bubbling, return chops to skillet. Cover, and reduce heat to low. Simmer for 20
   minutes, or until chops are cooked through.

SLOW COOKER CHICKEN CREOLE

Servings: 4 | Prep: 10m | Cooks: 12h | Total: 12h10m

NUTRITION FACTS

Calories: 189.2 | Carbohydrates: 13.8g | Protein: 29.6g | Cholesterol: 68.4mg | Sodium: 430.5mg

INGREDIENTS

- 4 skinless, boneless chicken breast halves
- salt and pepper to taste
- Creole-style seasoning to taste
- 1 (14.5 ounce) can stewed tomatoes, with liquid
- 1 stalk celery, diced
- 1 green bell pepper, diced
- 3 cloves garlic, minced
- 1 onion, diced
- 1 (4 ounce) can mushrooms, drained
- 1 fresh jalapeno pepper, seeded and chopped

DIRECTIONS

1. Place chicken breasts in slow cooker. Season with salt, pepper, and Creole-style seasoning to taste. Stir in tomatoes with liquid, celery, bell pepper, garlic, onion, mushrooms, and jalapeno pepper.
2. Cook on Low for 10 to 12 hours, or on High for 5 to 6 hours.

EASY MUSHROOM RICE

Servings: 4 | Prep: 5m | Cooks: 1h | Total: 1h5m

NUTRITION FACTS

Calories: 336.3 | Carbohydrates: 45.4g | Protein: 9.1g | Cholesterol: 33.4mg | Sodium: 1215.8mg

INGREDIENTS

- 1 cup uncooked long-grain rice
- 1 (10.5 ounce) can condensed French onion soup
- 1 (10.5 ounce) can beef broth
- 1 (4 ounce) can sliced mushrooms, drained
- 1/4 cup butter

DIRECTIONS

1. Preheat oven to 350 degrees F (175 degrees C).
2. Combine rice, onion soup, beef broth, mushrooms and butter in an 8x8 inch casserole dish.
3. Cover, and bake in the preheated oven for 60 minutes.

BAKED MUSHROOM THIGHS

Servings: 4 | Prep: 15m | Cooks: 45m | Total: 1h

NUTRITION FACTS

Calories: 574.9 | Carbohydrates: 29g | Protein: 39g | Cholesterol: 138.3mg | Sodium: 868mg

INGREDIENTS

- 8 chicken thighs
- 1 (10.75 ounce) can condensed cream of mushroom soup
- 10 ounces milk
- 1 teaspoon dried parsley
- 1/2 teaspoon onion powder
- 1 cup dry bread crumbs
- 2 tablespoons melted butter
- 1 teaspoon cornstarch

DIRECTIONS

1. Preheat oven to 350 degrees F (175 degrees C).
2. Pour the soup into a medium bowl. Fill the empty can with milk, and add to the bowl along with the parsley and onion powder. Mix well. Place bread crumbs in a shallow dish or bowl; dip chicken thighs in soup mixture, then in crumbs, and place coated pieces in a lightly greased 9x13 inch baking dish.
3. Drizzle with melted butter and bake in preheated oven until chicken is nicely browned and cooked through (juices run clear), about 45 minutes.
4. Meanwhile, place remaining soup mixture in a small saucepan and whisk in cornstarch. Cook over medium heat, stirring occasionally, until mixture comes to a boil; reduce heat and simmer for a minute or two until sauce thickens. Use this as a sauce when chicken is done.

CHICKEN WITH MUSHROOMS, PROSCIUTTO, AND CREAM SAUCE

Servings: 6 | Prep: 10m | Cooks: 1h | Total: 1h10m

NUTRITION FACTS

Calories: 382.8 | Carbohydrates: 3.3g | Protein: 20.7g | Cholesterol: 118.7mg | Sodium: 424.5mg

INGREDIENTS

- 2 tablespoons butter or margarine, melted
- 6 chicken thighs
- 1 pinch salt and pepper to taste
- 6 slices prosciutto (thin sliced)
- 2 tablespoons minced garlic, divided
- 1 cup sliced fresh mushrooms
- 1/4 cup dry white wine
- 1 cup sour cream

DIRECTIONS

1. Preheat oven to 350 degrees F (175 degrees C).
2. Drizzle butter into a casserole dish. Season chicken with salt, pepper, and 1 tablespoon garlic. Wrap chicken thighs in prosciutto, and place in casserole dish. Sprinkle mushrooms and remaining garlic on top of chicken.
3. Bake in a preheated oven until juices run clear, about 1 hour. Remove chicken to a platter, and cover with aluminum foil to keep warm.
4. Pour drippings from casserole into a skillet set over medium-low heat. Whisk in wine and sour cream, and cook until warmed through, about 5 to 7 minutes. Pour over chicken, and serve.

SPICY BASIL CHICKEN

Servings: 4 | Prep: 15m | Cooks: 15m | Total: 30m

NUTRITION FACTS

Calories: 244.1 | Carbohydrates: 11.9g | Protein: 28.2g | Cholesterol: 69.3mg | Sodium: 656.5mg

INGREDIENTS

- 2 tablespoons chili oil
- 2 cloves garlic
- 3 hot chile peppers
- 1 teaspoon black pepper
- 5 tablespoons oyster sauce
- 1 cup fresh mushrooms

* 1 pound skinless, boneless chicken breast halves - cut into bite-size pieces
* 1 1/2 teaspoons white sugar
* 1 teaspoon garlic salt
* 1 cup chopped onions
* 1 bunch fresh basil leaves

DIRECTIONS

1. Heat the oil in a skillet over medium-high heat, and cook the garlic and chile peppers until golden brown. Mix in chicken and sugar, and season with garlic salt and pepper. Cook until chicken is no longer pink, but not done.
2. Stir oyster sauce into the skillet. Mix in mushrooms and onions, and continue cooking until onions are tender and chicken juices run clear. Remove from heat, and mix in basil. Let sit 2 minutes before serving.

BARLEY BAKE

Servings: 6 | Prep: 25m | Cooks: 1h25m | Total: 1h50m

NUTRITION FACTS

Calories: 280 | Carbohydrates: 33.2g | Protein: 7.4g | Cholesterol: 20.3mg | Sodium: 437.5mg

INGREDIENTS

* 1/4 cup butter
* 1 medium onion, diced
* 1 cup uncooked pearl barley
* 1/2 cup pine nuts
* 2 green onions, thinly sliced
* 1/2 cup sliced fresh mushrooms
* 1/2 cup chopped fresh parsley
* 1/4 teaspoon salt
* 1/8 teaspoon pepper
* 2 (14.5 ounce) cans vegetable broth

DIRECTIONS

1. Preheat oven to 350 degrees F (175 degrees C).
2. Melt butter in a skillet over medium-high heat. Stir in onion, barley, and pine nuts. Cook and stir until barley is lightly browned. Mix in green onions, mushrooms, and parsley. Season with salt and pepper. Transfer the mixture to a 2 quart casserole dish, and stir in the vegetable broth.

3. Bake 1 hour and 15 minutes in the preheated oven, or until liquid has been absorbed and barley is tender.

MUSHROOM BLUE CHEESE TURKEY BURGERS

Servings: 4 | Prep: 15m | Cooks: 10m | Total: 25m

NUTRITION FACTS

Calories: 224.6 | Carbohydrates: 5.3g | Protein: 26.8g | Cholesterol: 90.2mg | Sodium: 876.7mg

INGREDIENTS

- 1 pound ground turkey
- 8 ounces fresh mushrooms, finely chopped
- 1 onion, finely chopped
- 2 tablespoons soy sauce
- 1/2 teaspoon kosher salt
- 1/4 teaspoon black pepper
- 1/4 cup crumbled blue cheese

DIRECTIONS

1. Preheat grill for high heat.
2. In a medium bowl, mix together the ground turkey, mushrooms, onion, and soy sauce. Season with kosher salt and pepper. Form into 4 burger patties.
3. Lightly oil the grill grate. Place patties on the prepared grill, and cook for 10 minutes per side, or until well done. Top with blue cheese during the last few minutes.

BACON MUSHROOM SWISS MEATLOAF

Servings: 6 | Prep: 20m | Cooks: 1h15m | Total: 1h35m

NUTRITION FACTS

Calories: 695.8 | Carbohydrates: 11.4g | Protein: 38.3g | Cholesterol: 177.1mg | Sodium: 683.2mg

INGREDIENTS

- 12 ounces chopped raw bacon
- 1 small white onion, chopped
- 5 button mushrooms, chopped
- 1 egg
- 1/4 cup evaporated milk
- 6 ounces shredded Swiss cheese, divided

- 1 1/2 pounds extra-lean ground beef
- 1/2 cup corn flake crumbs

DIRECTIONS

1. Preheat oven to 350 degrees F (175 degrees C).
2. Place bacon in a skillet and cook over medium heat until the pieces are browned. Remove with a slotted spoon to paper towels. Discard all but 1 tablespoon of bacon grease. Stir in onions and mushrooms, and cook until soft. Remove from heat.
3. In a large bowl, stir together beef, egg, and milk. Stir in the onion and mushrooms. Mix in about 4 ounces of Swiss cheese, and all but 1 tablespoon of bacon. Stir in cornflake crumbs, and mix until well blended. Shape into a loaf, and place in a meatloaf pan.
4. Bake in a preheated oven for 1 hour. Drain fat, and sprinkle with remaining cheese and bacon. Return to oven, and bake until cheese is melted, about 5 minutes.

CRAB STUFFED MUSHROOMS

Servings: 6 | Prep: 25m | Cooks: 15m | Total: 40m

NUTRITION FACTS

Calories: 167.1 | Carbohydrates: 4.2g | Protein: 11.7g | Cholesterol: 39.2mg | Sodium: 274.6mg

INGREDIENTS

- 1 pound fresh mushrooms
- 7 ounces crabmeat
- 5 green onions, thinly sliced
- 1/4 teaspoon dried thyme
- 1/4 teaspoon dried oregano
- 1/4 teaspoon ground savory
- ground black pepper to taste
- 1/4 cup grated Parmesan cheese
- 1/3 cup mayonnaise
- 3 tablespoons grated Parmesan cheese
- 1/4 teaspoon paprika

DIRECTIONS

1. Preheat the oven to 350 degrees F (175 degrees C).
2. In a medium bowl, combine crabmeat, green onions, herbs, and pepper. Mix in mayonnaise and 1/4 cup Parmesan cheese until well combined. Refrigerate filling until ready for use.
3. Wipe the mushrooms clean with a damp towel. Remove stems. Spoon out the gills and the base of the stem, making deep cups. Discard gills and stems. Fill the mushroom caps with rounded

teaspoonfuls of filling, and place them in an ungreased shallow baking dish. Sprinkle tops with Parmesan and paprika.

4. Bake for 15 minutes. Remove from oven, and serve immediately.

EASY SALMON

Servings: 6 | Prep: 15m | Cooks: 30m | Total: 45m

NUTRITION FACTS

Calories: 217.1 | Carbohydrates: 2.5g | Protein: 22.7g | Cholesterol: 66.1mg | Sodium: 597.4mg

INGREDIENTS

- 6 (4 ounce) fillets salmon
- 1 (.7 ounce) package dry Italian-style salad dressing mix
- 1/2 cup water
- 2 tablespoons lemon juice
- 1 cup fresh sliced mushrooms

DIRECTIONS

1. Preheat oven to 350 degrees F (175 degrees C). Lightly butter one 9x13 inch baking dish.
2. In a cup, combine salad dressing mix, water and lemon juice.
3. Arrange salmon fillets in a single layer in the prepared baking dish. Pour the water mixture over the top and place the sliced mushrooms over the salmon.
4. Bake, covered, for 15 minutes. Remove cover and bake for an additional 15 minutes, basting with cooking liquids.

SLOW COOKER CHICKEN PARISIENNE

Servings: 6 | Prep: 10m | Cooks: 8h | Total: 8h10m

NUTRITION FACTS

Calories: 296.3 | Carbohydrates: 10.6g | Protein: 30.2g | Cholesterol: 85.3mg | Sodium: 515.3mg

INGREDIENTS

- 6 skinless, boneless chicken breast halves
- salt and pepper to taste
- 1 (10.75 ounce) can condensed cream of mushroom soup
- 1 (4.5 ounce) can sliced mushrooms, drained

- paprika to taste
- 1/2 cup dry white wine
- 1 cup sour cream
- 1/4 cup all-purpose flour

DIRECTIONS

1. Sprinkle chicken breasts lightly with salt, pepper, and paprika to taste. Place in slow cooker.
2. In a mixing bowl, combine the wine, condensed soup, and mushrooms. In another bowl, mix together sour cream and flour. Stir sour cream mixture into the mushrooms and wine. Pour over chicken in slow cooker. Sprinkle with additional paprika, if desired.
3. Cover, and cook on Low for 6 to 8 hours.

CREAMY MUSHROOM SOUP

Servings: 4 | Prep: 10m | Cooks: 15m | Total: 25m

NUTRITION FACTS

Calories: 233.9 | Carbohydrates: 13.3g | Protein: 4.4g | Cholesterol: 52.9mg | Sodium: 119.3mg

INGREDIENTS

- 1/4 cup butter
- 1 cup chopped shiitake mushrooms
- 1 cup chopped portobello mushrooms
- 2 eaches shallots, chopped
- 2 tablespoons all-purpose flour
- 1 (14.5 ounce) can chicken broth
- 1 cup half-and-half
- salt and pepper to taste
- 1 pinch ground cinnamon

DIRECTIONS

1. Melt the butter in a large saucepan over medium-high heat. Saute the shiitake mushrooms, portobello mushrooms, and shallots for about 5 minutes, or until soft. Mix in the flour until smooth. Gradually stir in the chicken broth. Cook, stirring, 5 minutes, or until thick and bubbly.
2. Stir in the half-and-half, season with salt and pepper, and sprinkle with cinnamon. Heat through, but do not boil.

SAUTEED PORTOBELLOS AND SPINACH

Servings: 4 | Prep: 10m | Cooks: 10m | Total: 20m

NUTRITION FACTS

Calories: 146.3 | Carbohydrates: 6.6g | Protein: 6.6g | Cholesterol: 28.4mg | Sodium: 358.7mg

INGREDIENTS

- 3 tablespoons butter
- 2 large portobello mushrooms, sliced
- 1 (10 ounce) package frozen chopped spinach, thawed and drained
- 1/4 teaspoon dried basil
- 1/4 teaspoon salt
- 1/4 teaspoon black pepper
- 1 clove garlic, chopped
- 2 tablespoons dry red wine
- 1/4 cup grated Parmesan cheese

DIRECTIONS

1. Melt butter in a large skillet or saute pan over medium heat. Saute mushrooms, spinach, basil, salt, pepper and garlic until mushrooms are tender and spinach is heated through.
2. Pour in wine and reduce heat to low; simmer 1 minute. Stir in Parmesan cheese and serve.

BLACKENED SHRIMP STROGANOFF

Servings: 4 | Prep: 30m | Cooks: 30m | Total: 1h

NUTRITION FACTS

Calories: 440 | Carbohydrates: 41.4g | Fat: 16.1g | Protein: 33.1g | Cholesterol: 195mg

Sodium: 1208mg

INGREDIENTS

- 1 pound fresh shrimp, peeled and deveined
- 1 tablespoon olive oil
- 1 tablespoon Cajun seasoning
- 6 ounces fettuccini pasta
- 2/3 cup chicken broth
- 1/2 cup sour cream
- 1 tablespoon cornstarch
- 1 cup chicken broth

- 1 tablespoon butter
- 3 cups fresh mushrooms, sliced
- 1 tablespoon chopped shallots
- 1 (7 ounce) jar roasted red bell peppers
- 1 tablespoon drained capers

DIRECTIONS

1. Combine peeled shrimp, oil, and Cajun seasoning in a medium bowl. Set aside.
2. Bring a large pot of lightly salted water to a boil. Add pasta and cook for 8 to 10 minutes or until al dente; drain.
3. Meanwhile, melt butter over medium heat in a large frying pan. Cook and stir mushrooms and shallot in butter until tender. Remove from pan. Add shrimp cook until shrimp turn pink about 2 to 3 minutes. Remove from pan. Add 2/3 cup chicken broth to pan, and bring to a boil. Cook, uncovered, until reduced to 1/4 cup (2 to 3 minutes).
4. In a small bowl, stir together sour cream and cornstarch; mix in 1 cup chicken broth. Stir into reduced chicken broth in the frying pan. Cook and stir until thick and bubbly. Cook 1 minute more. Stir in shrimp, mushroom mixture, roasted red peppers, and capers. Heat through, and season to taste. Serve over pasta.

TERIYAKI AND PINEAPPLE CHICKEN

Servings: 8 | Prep: 15m | Cooks: 25m | Total: 40m

NUTRITION FACTS

Calories: 186.9 | Carbohydrates: 18.1g | Protein: 16.3g | Cholesterol: 34.6mg | Sodium: 1412.6mg

INGREDIENTS

- 2 tablespoons vegetable oil
- 1 pound skinless, boneless chicken breasts, cut into cubes
- 1 green bell pepper, sliced thin
- 1 yellow bell pepper, sliced thin
- 1 red bell pepper, sliced thin
- 1 1/4 cups sliced fresh mushrooms
- 1 onion, chopped
- 1 cup teriyaki sauce
- 1 (8 ounce) can pineapple chunks, undrained
- 1 teaspoon garlic powder
- 1 teaspoon crushed red pepper
- 1/4 cup all-purpose flour

DIRECTIONS

1. Heat the oil in a wok or large skillet over medium-high heat. Cook the chicken until no longer pink in the center and the juices run clear, 7 to 10 minutes.
2. Place the green bell pepper, yellow bell pepper, red bell pepper, mushrooms, onion, teriyaki sauce, pineapple chunks with the juice, garlic powder, and crushed red pepper into the wok, and turn the heat to medium. Bring to a simmer, stir in the flour, and continue simmering 15 minutes until thickened.

FETTUCCINI WITH MUSHROOM, HAM AND ROSE SAUCE
Servings: 8 | Prep: 15m | Cooks: 15m | Total: 30m

NUTRITION FACTS

Calories: 477.9 | Carbohydrates: 53.2g | Protein: 11.9g | Cholesterol: 77mg | Sodium: 191.6mg

INGREDIENTS

- 1 pound dry fettuccine pasta
- 1/4 cup butter
- 1/2 cup finely diced onion
- 3 cloves garlic, minced
- 1 pound fresh sliced mushrooms
- 2 teaspoons dried oregano
- 2 teaspoons dried basil
- 2 teaspoons dried parsley
- 6 slices ham, chopped
- 1 1/2 cups heavy whipping cream
- 1 cup spaghetti sauce
- 1 teaspoon crushed red pepper

DIRECTIONS

1. Bring a large pot of lightly salted water to a boil. Add pasta and cook for 8 to 10 minutes or until al dente; drain.
2. In a large saute pan, melt the butter over medium heat. Add the onion and garlic and cook until softened. Stir in the sliced mushrooms and the oregano, basil, and parsley. Cook, stirring occasionally, until the liquid from the mushrooms has evaporated. Add the ham pieces and cook for another 4 to 5 minutes.
3. Pour in the heavy cream and bring to a boil. Slowly stir in the spaghetti sauce and crushed red pepper blending it into the cream. Cook, stirring occasionally, until the sauce has reduced by a third and is thick.
4. Place fettuccini on plates and ladle even portions of sauce over top.

SAUSAGE STUFFED MUSHROOMS

Servings: 10 | Prep: 20m | Cooks: 3m | Total: 23m

NUTRITION FACTS

Calories: 177.8 | Carbohydrates: 1.6g | Protein: 5g | Cholesterol: 40.1mg | Sodium: 218.8mg

INGREDIENTS

- 1/2 pound ground pork sausage
- 1 (8 ounce) package fresh mushrooms, stems removed
- 1 (8 ounce) package cream cheese, softened

DIRECTIONS

1. Preheat the broiler.
2. Place sausage in a large, deep skillet. Cook over medium high heat until evenly brown. Drain and transfer to a medium bowl.
3. Blend cream cheese with the sausage. Stuff mushroom caps with the cream cheese and sausage mixture.
4. Arrange stuffed mushroom caps on a medium baking sheet. Broil in the preheated oven 2 to 3 minutes, until lightly browned.

PORTOBELLO SANDWICHES

Servings: 4 | Prep: 8m | Cooks: 9m | Total: 20m | Additional: 3m

NUTRITION FACTS

Calories: 445.1 | Carbohydrates: 31.4g | Protein: 7.8g | Cholesterol: 5.2mg | Sodium: 426mg

INGREDIENTS

- 2 cloves garlic, minced
- 6 tablespoons olive oil
- 1/2 teaspoon dried thyme
- 2 tablespoons balsamic vinegar
- salt and pepper to taste
- 4 large portobello mushroom caps
- 4 hamburger buns
- 1 tablespoon capers
- 1/4 cup mayonnaise
- 1 tablespoon capers, drained
- 1 large tomato, sliced
- 4 leaves lettuce

DIRECTIONS

1. Turn on broiler, and adjust rack so it is as close to heat source as possible.
2. In a medium-size mixing bowl, mix together garlic, olive oil, thyme, vinegar, salt and pepper.
3. Put the mushroom caps, bottom side up, in a shallow baking pan. Brush the caps with 1/2 the dressing. Put the caps under the broiler, and cook for 5 minutes.
4. Turn the caps, and brush with the remaining dressing. Broil 4 minutes. Toast the buns lightly .
5. In a small bowl, mix capers and mayonnaise. Spread mayonnaise mixture on the buns, top with mushroom caps, tomato and lettuce.

CRAB-STUFFED FILET MIGNON WITH WHISKEY PEPPERCORN SAUCE

Servings: 4 | Prep: 1h | Cooks: 30m | Total: 1h30m

NUTRITION FACTS

Calories: 748.4 | Carbohydrates: 6.7g | Protein: 41.4g | Cholesterol: 215.4mg | Sodium: 1175.4mg

INGREDIENTS

- 2 tablespoons olive oil
- 1 teaspoon minced onion
- 1 teaspoon minced green onion
- 1 teaspoon minced garlic
- 1 teaspoon minced celery
- 1 teaspoon minced green bell pepper
- 2 tablespoons shrimp stock or water
- 1 (6 ounce) can crab meat, drained
- 2 tablespoons bread crumbs
- 1 teaspoon Cajun seasoning
- 1 1/4 cups beef broth
- 1 teaspoon cracked black pepper
- 1 fluid ounce whiskey
- 1 cup heavy cream
- 4 (6 ounce) filet mignon steaks
- 4 slices bacon, cooked lightly
- 1/2 teaspoon salt and cracked black pepper to taste
- 1 tablespoon olive oil
- 1 clove garlic, minced
- 1 teaspoon minced shallot
- 1 cup crimini mushrooms, sliced
- 1 fluid ounce whiskey
- 1 teaspoon Dijon mustard

DIRECTIONS

1. Make Crab Stuffing: Heat 2 tablespoons olive oil in a large skillet. Saute onion, green onion, garlic, celery, and green pepper until tender. Stir in shrimp stock, crab meat, bread crumbs, and Cajun seasoning. Remove from heat, and set aside.

2. Prepare Peppercorn Sauce: In a small saucepan over medium heat, combine beef broth and cracked black pepper. Simmer until reduced to 1 cup, stirring frequently. Add1 ounce whiskey and 1 cup cream. Continue simmering until reduced to 1 cup. Remove from heat, and set aside.

3. Prepare Steaks: Slice a pocket into the side of each steak, and stuff generously with crab stuffing. Wrap bacon around side, and secure with toothpicks. Season to taste with salt and pepper; set aside. Heat olive oil in a large cast iron skillet over medium heat. Saute garlic and shallot for 1 minute. Stir in mushrooms, and saute until tender. Remove mushroom mixture, and set aside.

4. Place steaks in skillet, and cook to desired doneness. Remove from skillet, and keep warm. Deglaze skillet with 1 ounce whiskey. Reduce heat, and stir in peppercorn sauce and Dijon mustard. Add mushroom mixture, and reduce sauce until thickened. Remove toothpicks and bacon from steaks, and arrange steaks on a plate. Top with sauce.

MUSHROOM LENTIL BARLEY STEW
Servings: 8 | Prep: 15m | Cooks: 12h | Total: 12h15m

NUTRITION FACTS

Calories: 213 | Carbohydrates: 43.9g | Fat: 1.2g | Protein: 8.4g | Cholesterol: 0mg | Sodium: 466mg

INGREDIENTS

- 2 quarts vegetable broth
- 2 cups sliced fresh button mushrooms
- 1 ounce dried shiitake mushrooms, torn into pieces
- 3/4 cup uncooked pearl barley
- 3/4 cup dry lentils
- 1/4 cup dried onion flakes
- 2 teaspoons minced garlic
- 2 teaspoons dried summer savory
- 3 bay leaves
- 1 teaspoon dried basil
- 2 teaspoons ground black pepper
- salt to taste

DIRECTIONS

1. In a slow cooker, mix the broth, button mushrooms, shiitake mushrooms, barley, lentils, onion flakes, garlic, savory, bay leaves, basil, pepper, and salt.

2. Cover, and cook 4 to 6 hours on High or 10 to 12 hours on Low. Remove bay leaves before serving.

CHICKEN DANIELLE

Servings: 4 | Prep: 15m | Cooks: 1h15m | Total: 1h30m

NUTRITION FACTS

Calories: 1005.4 | Carbohydrates: 81.1g | Protein: 43.5g | Cholesterol: 196.7mg | Sodium: 1258.5mg

INGREDIENTS

- 8 tablespoons butter, divided
- 4 skinless, boneless chicken breast halves
- salt and pepper to taste
- 6 ounces button mushrooms, sliced
- 3/4 cup Marsala wine, divided
- 1 (10.75 ounce) can condensed cream of chicken soup
- 1 (10.75 ounce) can condensed cream of mushroom soup
- 3/4 cup heavy cream
- 1/2 teaspoon chopped fresh rosemary
- 1/4 teaspoon chopped fresh thyme
- 1 (12 ounce) package uncooked linguine pasta

DIRECTIONS

1. Melt 6 tablespoons butter in a large skillet over medium high heat. Season chicken with salt and pepper and add to skillet. Cook until halfway done and golden brown on both sides, about 4 to 7 minutes each side. When browned, remove chicken to a 9x13 inch baking dish. Set skillet aside, reserving drippings.
2. In a separate skillet, melt the 2 remaining tablespoons of butter over medium high heat and saute mushrooms. Add 1/4 cup of the wine and stir; let reduce over low heat for 5 minutes. Set mushrooms and drippings aside, keeping warm.
3. Preheat oven to 375 degrees F (190 degrees C).
4. Add cream of chicken soup and cream of mushroom soup to reserved chicken/drippings skillet. Mix soups well with drippings, making sure no lumps remain. Slowly add cream, stirring constantly, then add remaining 1/2 cup wine; season with rosemary and thyme. Adjust amount of wine as needed to make a nice, thick gravy consistency. Let mixture simmer over medium heat until bubbly, then add reserved mushroom mixture and stir together.
5. Pour soup/mushroom mixture over chicken in baking dish, cover and bake in preheated oven for 30 to 45 minutes.
6. About 15 minutes before serving chicken, bring a large pot of lightly salted water to a boil. Add linguine and cook for 8 to 10 minutes or until al dente; drain. Serve chicken breasts and sauce over the hot cooked pasta.

PASTA WITH ASPARAGUS

Servings: 4 | Prep: 15m | Cooks: 10m | Total: 25m

NUTRITION FACTS

Calories: 280.7 | Carbohydrates: 39.4g | Protein: 15.5g | Cholesterol: 8.8mg | Sodium: 338.6mg

INGREDIENTS

- 1 1/2 pounds fresh asparagus, trimmed and cut into 1 inch pieces
- 1/4 cup chicken broth
- 1/2 pound fresh mushrooms, sliced
- 8 ounces angel hair pasta
- 1 tablespoon olive oil
- 1/2 teaspoon crushed red pepper
- 1/2 cup grated Parmesan cheese

DIRECTIONS

1. Cook pasta according to package instructions.
2. Heat the olive oil in a nonstick skillet. Saute asparagus in the pan over medium heat for about 3 minutes. Add chicken broth and mushroom slices; cook 3 minutes more.
3. Drain pasta, and transfer to a serving dish. Gently toss pasta with asparagus mixture; sprinkle with Parmesan and crushed red pepper.

FABULOUS FAJITAS

Servings: 10 | Prep: 15m | Cooks: 15m | Total: 30m

NUTRITION FACTS

Calories: 427.2 | Carbohydrates: 64.2g | Protein: 18g | Cholesterol: 21mg | Sodium: 1078.5mg

INGREDIENTS

- 2 green bell peppers, sliced
- 1 red bell pepper, sliced
- 1 onion, thinly sliced
- 1 cup fresh sliced mushrooms
- 2 cups diced, cooked chicken meat
- 1 (.7 ounce) package dry Italian-style salad dressing mix
- 10 (12 inch) flour tortillas

DIRECTIONS

1. Cut peppers and onion into thin slices. Do not dice, leave slices long and thin.
2. Saute peppers and onion in a small amount of oil until tender. Add mushrooms and chicken. Continue to cook on low heat until heated through. Stir in dry salad dressing mix and blend thoroughly.
3. Warm tortillas and roll mixture inside. If desired top with shredded cheddar cheese, diced tomato and shredded lettuce.

SLOW COOKER PORK CACCIATORE

Servings: 4 | Prep: 15m | Cooks: 8h30m | Total: 8h45m

NUTRITION FACTS

Calories: 614 | Carbohydrates: 41.8g | Fat: 31g | Protein: 34.5g | Cholesterol: 82mg | Sodium: 1485mg

INGREDIENTS

- 2 tablespoons olive oil
- 1 onion, sliced
- 4 boneless pork chops
- 1 (28 ounce) jar pasta sauce
- 1 (28 ounce) can diced tomatoes
- 1 green bell pepper, seeded and sliced into strips
- 1 (8 ounce) package fresh mushrooms, sliced
- 2 large cloves garlic, minced
- 1 teaspoon Italian seasoning
- 1/2 teaspoon dried basil
- 1/2 cup dry white wine
- 4 slices mozzarella cheese

DIRECTIONS

1. In a large skillet, brown chops over medium-high heat. Transfer to slow cooker.
2. In the same pan, cook onion in oil over medium heat until browned. Stir in mushrooms and bell pepper, and cook until these vegetables are soft. Mix in pasta sauce, diced tomatoes, and white wine. Season with Italian seasoning, basil, and garlic. Pour over pork chops in slow cooker.
3. Cook on Low for 7 to 8 hours. To serve, place a slice of cheese over each chop, and cover with sauce.

CHICKEN AND BOWTIE PASTA WITH ASIAGO CREAM SAUCE

Servings: 6 | Prep: 20m | Cooks: 40m | Total: 1h

NUTRITION FACTS

Calories: 836.6 | Carbohydrates: 61.5g | Protein: 33.2g | Cholesterol: 192.1mg | Sodium: 424.6mg

INGREDIENTS

- 1 (16 ounce) package farfalle (bow tie) pasta
- 2 tablespoons vegetable oil
- 1 pound skinless, boneless chicken breast halves - cubed
- 2 1/4 cups heavy cream, divided
- 1/4 cube chicken bouillon, crumbled
- 3/4 cup grated Asiago cheese
- 1/2 tablespoon cornstarch
- 2 tablespoons butter
- 1/4 cup chopped prosciutto
- 1 tablespoon chopped fresh garlic
- 1/4 cup sliced mushrooms
- 1/2 tablespoon parsley flakes

DIRECTIONS

1. Bring a large pot of lightly salted water to a boil. Cook pasta for 8 to 10 minutes, or until al dente. Drain, and set aside.
2. Heat 2 tablespoons vegetable oil in a skillet over medium-high heat. Cook and stir chicken cubes, reducing heat if necessary, until no longer pink in center and juices run clear. Set aside.
3. In a medium saucepan, bring 2 cups cream to a simmer, stirring often. Whisk in bouillon and cheese until well blended and bouillon has dissolved completely. Dissolve cornstarch in 2 tablespoons water, and whisk into mixture. Cook and stir 2 minutes more, then remove from heat and set aside.
4. Melt butter in a medium skillet over medium high heat. Stir in prosciutto, garlic, and mushrooms and cook until mushrooms are tender, about 3 minutes. Add chicken, reduce heat, and continue cooking until chicken is heated through. Return sauce to the stove and add remaining 1/4 cup cream and parsley flakes. Heat through.
5. To serve, place pasta in a large mixing or serving bowl. Add chicken and mushroom mixture and pour in cream sauce. Toss well, and serve.

AMAZING PORK CHOPS IN CREAM SAUCE

Servings: 8 | Prep: 10m | Cooks: 15m | Total: 25m

NUTRITION FACTS

Calories: 349 | Carbohydrates: 2.5g | Protein: 24.5g | Cholesterol: 105.1mg | Sodium: 85.9mg

INGREDIENTS

- 3 tablespoons butter
- 8 eaches boneless pork chops
- 1 pinch salt, to taste
- 1 pinch ground black pepper, to taste
- 3/4 cup white wine
- 3/4 cup heavy cream
- 1 (8 ounce) package sliced fresh mushrooms

DIRECTIONS

1. Melt butter in a large skillet over medium heat. Season pork chops with salt and pepper, and arrange in a single layer in pan. Pan-fry for 2 minutes on each side to brown. Pour in wine, and continue cooking for 6 minutes. Remove chops from pa
2. Pour cream into the skillet, and then add mushrooms. Increase heat to high; cook for 5 minutes, stirring frequently, until sauce reduces and thickens. Return chops to pan to warm before serving.

CHEESY ACORN SQUASH

Servings: 2 | Prep: 15m | Cooks: 40m | Total: 55m

NUTRITION FACTS

Calories: 413.5 | Carbohydrates: 35.8g | Protein: 11.9g | Cholesterol: 75.5mg | Sodium: 504.3mg

INGREDIENTS

- 1 acorn squash, halved and seeded
- 3 tablespoons butter
- 1 cup diced celery
- 1 cup finely chopped onion
- 1 cup fresh mushrooms, sliced
- 1/8 teaspoon salt
- 1 pinch ground black pepper
- 1 teaspoon chopped parsley
- 1/2 cup shredded Cheddar chees

DIRECTIONS

1. Preheat oven to 350 degrees F (175 degrees C).
2. Place squash cut side down in a glass dish. Cook in microwave for 20 minutes on high, until almost tender.
3. In a saucepan over medium heat, melt butter and add celery and onion; saute until transparent. Stir in mushrooms; cook 2 to 3 minutes more. Sprinkle with salt, pepper, and parsley. Divide mixture in half, spoon into the squash and cover.
4. Cook 15 minutes in the preheated 350 degrees F (175 degrees C) oven. Uncover, sprinkle with cheese and put back in the oven until the cheese bubbles.

INSTANT POT MUSHROOM RISOTTO

Servings: 4 | Prep: 15m | Cooks: 30m | Total: 50m | Additional: 5m

NUTRITION FACTS

Calories: 644.9 | Carbohydrates: 76.6g | Protein: 12.4g | Cholesterol: 40mg | Sodium: 881.4mg

INGREDIENTS

- 1/4 cup unsalted butter
- 1/4 cup olive oil
- 3 cups diced mushrooms
- 1 cup chopped onion
- 1 sprig rosemary
- 1 1/2 cups Arborio rice
- 3/4 cup white wine
- 1 quart chicken stock
- 1 pinch salt and ground black pepper to taste
- 1/2 cup grated Parmesan cheese

DIRECTIONS

1. Select the Saute function on an electric pressure cooker (such as Instant Pot®). Add butter and olive oil; stir until butter melts, about 2 minutes. Add mushrooms; cook, stirring occasionally, until slightly softened, about 3 minutes. Stir in onion; cook for 2 minutes. Add rosemary sprig; cook for 1 minute.
2. Stir rice into the pot until each grain is coated with butter-olive oil mixture, about 2 minutes. Pour in wine; simmer for 3 minutes. Pour in chicken stock, stirring to scrape the sides of the pot. Simmer for 1 minute.
3. Close and lock the lid. Turn the venting knob to sealing. Select high pressure according to manufacturer's instructions; set timer for 6 minutes. Allow 10 to 15 minutes for pressure to build.
4. Tap venting knob a few times with a wooden spoon or spatula. Stand back; turn knob to point at Vent. Remove lid when pressure is released, about 5 minutes.

5. Stir risotto until creamy, about 1 minute. Discard rosemary sprig. Season with salt and pepper. Stir in Parmesan cheese until melted and combined.

CREAMY MUSHROOM PASTA

Servings: 6 | Prep: 15m | Cooks: 30m | Total: 45m

NUTRITION FACTS

Calories: 375 | Carbohydrates: 33.6g | Fat: 22.4g | Protein: 11.1g | Cholesterol: 61mg | Sodium: 371mg

INGREDIENTS

- 2 tablespoons olive oil
- 3//4 pound fresh white mushrooms, sliced
- 1/4 pound fresh shiitake mushrooms, stemmed and sliced
- salt and ground black pepper to taste
- 2 cloves garlic, minced
- 2 fluid ounces sherry
- 1 cup chicken stock
- 1 cup heavy whipping cream
- 8 ounces fettuccine pasta
- 1 1/2 teaspoons chopped fresh thyme
- 1 1/2 teaspoons chopped fresh chives
- 1 1/2 teaspoons chopped fresh tarragon
- 9 tablespoons freshly shredded Parmigiano-Reggiano cheese, divided

DIRECTIONS

1. Heat olive oil in a large skillet over medium heat. Cook and stir white and shiitake mushrooms in the hot oil with a pinch of salt until until the juice from the mushrooms evaporates and the mushrooms are browned, about 10 minutes.
2. Stir garlic into mushrooms and cook for 1 minute; pour in sherry and cook until wine is nearly evaporated. Mix chicken stock into mushroom mixture; season with salt and black pepper. Bring to a simmer, reduce heat, and cook until slightly thickened, about 5 minutes.
3. Pour cream into mushroom mixture, stir to combine, and simmer for 5 minutes. Mixture will foam and thicken slightly.
4. Fill a large pot with lightly salted water and bring to a rolling boil. Stir in the fettuccine, bring back to a boil, and cook pasta over medium heat until cooked through but still firm to the bite, about 8 minutes. Drain but do not rinse pasta; transfer to a large serving bowl and keep warm.
5. Stir thyme, chives, and tarragon into mushroom sauce and turn off heat; mix 1/2 cup Parmigiano-Reggiano cheese into sauce until cheese has melted.

6. Pour all the mushroom sauce and half the mushrooms over pasta, reserving about half the mushrooms in the skillet. Toss pasta in sauce until coated; top with remaining mushrooms and remaining 1 tablespoon Parmigiano-Reggiano cheese for garnish.

THE BEST STUFFED MUSHROOMS
Servings: 6 | Prep: 10m | Cooks: 40m | Total: 50m

NUTRITION FACTS

Calories: 161.5 | Carbohydrates: 3.5g | Protein: 6.7g | Cholesterol: 33mg | Sodium: 231.7mg

INGREDIENTS

- 3 slices bacon
- 1/2 (8 ounce) package cream cheese, softened
- 2 tablespoons grated Parmesan cheese
- 3 drops Worcestershire sauce
- 2 dashes ground black pepper
- 1 pound mushrooms, stems removed
- 2 tablespoons grated Parmesan cheese

DIRECTIONS

1. Preheat an oven to 350 degrees F (175 degrees C).
2. Place the bacon in a large, deep skillet and cook over medium-high heat, turning occasionally, until crisp and evenly browned, about 10 minutes. Drain the bacon slices on a paper towel-lined plate; crumble the drained bacon into a bowl. Stir in the cream cheese, 2 tablespoons Parmesan cheese, Worcestershire sauce, and pepper until evenly mixed. Spoon the filling into the mushroom caps and place into an 8x8-inch baking dish. Sprinkle with the remaining 2 tablespoons of Parmesan cheese.
3. Bake in the preheated oven until the mushrooms are tender and the filling is golden brown, 25 to 30 minutes.

ABSOLUTELY FABULOUS PORTOBELLO MUSHROOM TORTELLINI
Servings: 4 | Prep: 10m | Cooks: 15m | Total: 25m

NUTRITION FACTS

Calories: 469.5 | Carbohydrates: 42.2g | Protein: 18.3g | Cholesterol: 55mg | Sodium: 932.5mg

INGREDIENTS

- 1 pound cheese tortellini
- 2 large portobello mushrooms
- 1/4 cup white wine
- 1 tablespoon chopped fresh parsley
- 2 cloves garlic, minced
- 8 ounces Alfredo-style pasta sauce
- salt and pepper to taste
- 1/3 cup grated Parmesan cheese

DIRECTIONS

1. Bring a large pot of lightly salted water to a boil. Add pasta and cook for 8 to 10 minutes or until al dente; drain.
2. Meanwhile, prepare mushrooms by rinsing and thinly slicing the mushroom caps; discard the stems.
3. In a medium skillet over low heat, combine wine, parsley, garlic and mushrooms; stirring frequently, saute for approximately 5 minutes or until mushrooms are cooked through.
4. Remove skillet from heat and slowly add Alfredo sauce, stirring to blend; season with salt and pepper to taste.
5. Separate hot pasta into four portions and spoon sauce over pasta. Garnish with cheese and serve immediately.

VERY EASY MUSHROOM BARLEY SOUP

Servings: 6 | Prep: 15m | Cooks: 50m | Total: 1h5m

NUTRITION FACTS

Calories: 198 | Carbohydrates: 24g | Protein: 5.9g | Cholesterol: 0mg | Sodium: 27.7mg

INGREDIENTS

- 1/4 cup olive oil
- 1 cup chopped onion
- 3/4 cup diced carrots
- 1/2 cup chopped celery
- 1 teaspoon minced garlic
- 1 pound sliced fresh mushrooms
- 6 cups chicken broth
- 3/4 cup barley
- 1 pinch salt and pepper to taste

DIRECTIONS

1. Heat the oil in a large soup pot over medium heat. Add the onion, carrots, celery and garlic; cook and stir until onions are tender and transparent. Stir in mushrooms and continue to cook for a few minutes. Pour in the chicken broth and add barley. Bring to a boil, then reduce heat to low. Cover and simmer until barley is tender, about 50 minutes. Season with salt and pepper before serving.

CHICKEN BREASTS SUPREME

Servings: 6 | Prep: 25m | Cooks: 1h35m | Total: 2h

NUTRITION FACTS

Calories: 334.9 | Carbohydrates: 8.9g | Protein: 28.2g | Cholesterol: 100.2mg | Sodium: 768.6mg

INGREDIENTS

- 6 skinless, boneless chicken breast halves
- 1 pinch salt and pepper to taste
- 1 pinch paprika, or to taste
- 3 tablespoons butter
- 1 (10.75 ounce) can condensed cream of mushroom soup
- 1/3 cup milk
- 2 tablespoons minced onion
- ½ cup processed cheese (such as Velveeta®), diced
- 2 tablespoons Worcestershire sauce
- 1 (4.5 ounce) can sliced mushrooms, drained and chopped
- 2/3 cup sour cream

DIRECTIONS

1. Preheat oven to 350 degrees F (175 degrees C). Grease a 2-quart casserole dish.
2. Sprinkle the chicken breasts with salt, pepper, and paprika. Melt butter in a large skillet and brown the chicken breasts well on both sides, about 5 minutes per side. Lay the chicken breasts into the bottom of the prepared casserole dish.
3. In a saucepan over medium-low heat, mix together the mushroom soup, milk, onion, processed cheese, Worcestershire sauce, and mushrooms. Allow the mixture to heat until the cheese melts, but do not boil. Stir to thoroughly combine; mix in the sour cream until smooth. Pour the sauce over the chicken breasts in the dish and cover with foil.
4. Bake in the preheated oven until the chicken is tender and the juices run clear, about 45 minutes. Uncover, baste with sauce, and bake 30 more minutes, basting occasionally.

CHICKEN MONTEREY

Servings: 8 | Prep: 30m | Cooks: 55m | Total: 1h25m

NUTRITION FACTS

Calories: 399 | Carbohydrates: 16g | Protein: 32.6g | Cholesterol: 116.6mg | Sodium: 484.8mg

INGREDIENTS

- 1/2 cup butter, divided
- 1/2 cup chopped onion
- 8 large mushrooms, chopped
- 1 clove garlic, minced
- 2 tablespoons all-purpose flour
- 1/2 cup chicken stock
- 1 teaspoon celery salt
- 1/2 teaspoon white pepper
- 1/2 cup white wine
- 1 1/2 cups shredded Monterey Jack cheese
- 1 cup all-purpose flour
- salt and pepper to taste
- 8 skinless, boneless chicken breast halves - pounded thin

DIRECTIONS

1. Preheat oven to 300 degrees F (150 degrees C). Lightly grease a medium baking dish.
2. Melt 1/4 cup butter in a medium skillet over medium heat. Stir in onion, mushrooms and garlic. Cook until tender, about 10 minutes. Stir in 2 tablespoons flour, chicken stock, celery salt, white pepper and white wine. Reduce heat to low, and cook, stirring frequently, until thickened and well blended, about 10 minutes. Mix 1/2 cup Monterey Jack cheese into the thickened sauce mixture, and stir until melted.
3. In a shallow medium bowl, mix 1 cup flour with salt and pepper. Dredge chicken breast halves in the flour mixture to coat. Melt remaining 1/4 cup butter in a large skillet over medium high heat. Cook chicken until lightly browned on all sides. Arrange breast halves in the prepared baking dish, and cover with the sauce.
4. Top chicken breast halves with remaining Monterey Jack cheese. Bake in the preheated oven 25 minutes, or until chicken is no longer pink and juices run clear.

SHRIMPCARGOT

Servings: 3 | Prep: 15m | Cooks: 15m | Total: 30m

NUTRITION FACTS

Calories: 203 | Carbohydrates: 2.4g | Protein: 11.1g | Cholesterol: 107.5mg | Sodium: 202.4mg

INGREDIENTS

- 1/4 cup butter
- 2 cloves garlic, minced
- 6 eaches peeled and deveined large shrimp (21 to 25 per lb)
- 6 mushrooms, stems removed
- 2 tablespoons shredded mozzarella cheese

DIRECTIONS

1. Preheat oven to 325 degrees F (165 degrees C).
2. Heat the butter and garlic in a skillet over medium heat until the butter begins to bubble. Stir in the shrimp, and cook until they just turn pink, about 3 minutes. Place one shrimp into each mushroom cap, and place into a small baking dish. Spoon the garlic butter into the mushroom caps, and sprinkle each with a pinch of mozzarella cheese.
3. Bake in the preheated oven until the mushrooms are tender and the cheese is golden and bubbly, 10 to 15 minutes.

GRANDMA'S PORK CHOPS IN MUSHROOM GRAVY

Servings: 6 | Prep: 15m | Cooks: 1h | Total: 1h15m

NUTRITION FACTS

Calories: 208.7 | Carbohydrates: 10.7g | Protein: 19.2g | Cholesterol: 58.6mg | Sodium: 609mg

INGREDIENTS

- 1 tablespoon butter
- 1 clove garlic, pressed
- 6 pork chops
- 1 pinch salt and pepper to taste
- 1 (8 ounce) can
- 1 cup dry sherry
- 1 (10.5 ounce) can beef broth
- 2 tablespoons cornstarch
- 2 tablespoons water

mushrooms, drained

DIRECTIONS

1. Preheat the oven to 350 degrees F (175 degrees C).
2. Melt the butter in a large skillet over medium heat. Add garlic, and saute until fragrant. Season pork chops with salt and pepper, then fry them in the skillet just until browned on both sides, about 3 minutes per side. Remove the pork chops to a baking pan or Dutch oven.
3. Pour the mushrooms into the skillet with the pork drippings and garlic, and stir in the sherry and beef broth, scraping any bits of pork that are stuck to the pan. Bring to a boil, then pour over the pork chops in the baking pan. Cover with a lid, or aluminum foil.
4. Bake for 45 minutes in the preheated oven, then remove the lid or foil, and continue to bake for another 15 minutes. Remove the chops from the pan to a serving platter, and place the dish on the stove over medium heat. Stir together the cornstarch and water. When the juices in the pan come to a boil, slowly stir in the cornstarch mixture and cook until thickened, about 2 minutes. Spoon sauce over the chops, and serve.

COQ AU VIN ALLA ITALIANA
Servings: 8 | Prep: 10m | Cooks: 50m | Total: 1h

NUTRITION FACTS

Calories: 606.5 | Carbohydrates: 20.4g | Protein: 43.5g | Cholesterol: 149.7mg | Sodium: 518.5mg

INGREDIENTS

- 4 pounds dark meat chicken pieces
- 1 tablespoon vegetable oil
- 5 cloves crushed garlic
- 1/2 cup all-purpose flour
- 1 teaspoon poultry seasoning
- 3 (4 ounce) links sweet Italian sausage, sliced
- 1 cup chopped onion
- 3 carrots, sliced
- 1/2 pound fresh mushrooms, sliced
- 1/2 teaspoon dried rosemary
- 1 cup red wine
- 1 (14.5 ounce) can whole peeled tomatoes
- salt and pepper to taste

DIRECTIONS

1. In a large skillet, heat oil. Add 1/2 of the garlic. Season flour with poultry seasoning. Dredge chicken parts in flour, then brown in the skillet for 4 or 5 minutes. Add the sausage, and saute for a few minutes. Add the onion, carrots, mushrooms, rosemary and the remaining garlic. Stir all together.
2. Add the wine and tomatoes; stir. Cover and let simmer over low heat for 25 minutes. Season with salt and pepper to taste and let simmer for another 10 minutes. Let cool covered for 10 minutes, then serve.

STUFFED MUSHROOMS WITH SPINACH
Servings: 12 | Prep: 15m | Cooks: 30m | Total: 45m

NUTRITION FACTS

Calories: 162.5 | Carbohydrates: 2.5g | Protein: 4g | Cholesterol: 38.4mg | Sodium: 198.6mg

INGREDIENTS

- 2 tablespoons butter
- 5 slices bacon
- 1 (10 ounce) package frozen chopped spinach
- 12 large mushrooms
- 3 tablespoons butter
- 2 tablespoons finely chopped onion

- 2 cloves garlic, peeled and minced
- 4 cup heavy cream
- 1/4 cup grated Parmesan cheese
- salt and pepper to taste
- 2 tablespoons butter, melted

DIRECTIONS

1. Preheat oven to 400 degrees F (200 degrees C). Butter a 9x13 inch baking dish with 2 tablespoons butter.
2. Place bacon in a large, deep skillet. Cook over medium high heat until evenly brown. Drain, crumble and set aside.
3. Place frozen spinach in a medium saucepan with 1/4 cup water. Bring water to a boil, then reduce heat to medium and cook spinach covered 10 minutes. Uncover and stir. Remove from heat and drain.
4. Remove stems from mushrooms. Arrange caps in the baking dish. Finely chop stems.
5. Melt 3 tablespoons butter in a medium saucepan over medium heat, and mix in onion and garlic. Cook 5 minutes, or until tender, then mix in bacon, spinach, chopped mushroom stems and heavy cream. Bring cream to a boil. Remove from heat and mix in Parmesan cheese, salt and pepper.

6. Stuff mushroom caps generously with the mixture. Drizzle with 2 tablespoons melted butter. Bake in the preheated oven 30 minutes until lightly browned.

HERBED MUSHROOMS WITH WHITE WINE

Servings: 6 | Prep: 10m | Cooks: 15m | Total: 25m

NUTRITION FACTS

Calories: 56.5 | Carbohydrates: 5.6g | Protein: 2.3g | Cholesterol: 0mg | Sodium: 4.9mg

INGREDIENTS

- 1 tablespoon olive oil
- 1 1/2 pounds fresh mushrooms
- 1 teaspoon Italian seasoning
- 1/4 cup dry white wine
- 2 cloves garlic, minced
- 1 pinch salt and pepper to taste
- 2 tablespoons chopped fresh chives

DIRECTIONS

1. Heat the oil in a skillet over medium heat. Place mushrooms in the skillet, season with Italian seasoning, and cook 10 minutes, stirring frequently.
2. Mix the wine and garlic into the skillet, and continue cooking until most of the wine has evaporated. Season with salt and pepper, and sprinkle with chives. Continue cooking 1 minute.

SPINACH STUFFED PORTOBELLO MUSHROOMS

Servings: 4 | Prep: 15m | Cooks: 25m | Total: 40m

NUTRITION FACTS

Calories: 168.2 | Carbohydrates: 7.5g | Protein: 11.3g | Cholesterol: 70.4mg | Sodium: 590.5mg

INGREDIENTS

- 4 large portobello mushroom caps, stems and gills removed
- 1 tablespoon reduced-fat Italian salad dressing
- 1 egg
- 1 (10 ounce) bag fresh spinach, chopped
- 1/4 cup chopped pepperoni
- 1/4 cup grated Parmesan cheese

- 1 clove garlic, minced
- 1 pinch salt and ground black pepper to taste
- 1/4 cup shredded mozzarella cheese, divided
- 3 tablespoons seasoned bread crumbs, divided

DIRECTIONS

1. Preheat oven to 350 degrees F (175 degrees C).
2. Brush both sides of each portobello mushroom cap with Italian dressing. Arrange mushroom on a baking sheet, gill sides up.
3. Bake mushrooms in the preheated oven until tender, about 12 minutes. Drain any juice that has formed in the mushrooms.
4. Beat egg, garlic, salt, and black pepper together in a large bowl.
5. Stir spinach, pepperoni, Parmesan cheese, 3 tablespoons mozzarella cheese, and 3 tablespoons bread crumbs into the eggs until evenly mixed.
6. Divide spinach mixture over mushroom caps; sprinkle mushrooms with remaining 1 tablespoon mozzarella cheese and 1 tablespoon bread crumbs. Return mushrooms to the oven.
7. Continue baking until topping is golden brown and cheese is melted, about 10 minutes more.

MONTEREY CHICKEN

Servings: 4 | Prep: 45m | Cooks: 15m | Total: 3h | Additional: 2h

NUTRITION FACTS

Calories: 642.2 | Carbohydrates: 27.5g | Protein: 46.4g | Cholesterol: 140.2mg | Sodium: 2806.6mg

INGREDIENTS

- 4 skinless, boneless chicken breast halves
- 1 cup teriyaki marinade sauce
- 1/2 pound bacon
- 2 tablespoons butter
- 1 small onion, cut into long slices
- 1 small green bell pepper, cut into thin strips
- 1 (8 ounce) package fresh mushrooms, coarsely chopped
- 4 slices mozzarella cheese

DIRECTIONS

1. To Marinate: Place chicken in a nonporous glass dish or bowl. Pour marinade over chicken and toss to coat. Cover and refrigerate to marinate for 1 to 2 hours.
2. Preheat oven to 350 degrees F (175 degrees C).

3. Place chicken in a 9x13 inch baking dish and bake preheated oven for 20 to 30 minutes, or until cooked through and juices run clear. Meanwhile, place bacon in a large, deep skillet. Cook over medium high heat until evenly brown. Drain and set aside.

4. In same skillet, melt butter over medium high heat. Saute onion, bell pepper and mushrooms for about 3 to 5 minutes. Add remaining 1/3 cup of marinade and simmer until soft. Drain and set onion mixture aside.

5. Top baked chicken with bacon strips. Add onion mixture and top each breast with a slice of cheese. Bake for another 10 to 15 minutes, or until cheese is melted and bubbly.

MARINATED MUSHROOMS

Servings: 16 | Prep: 15m | Cooks: 12m | Total: 27m

NUTRITION FACTS

Calories: 54.1 | Carbohydrates: 2.8g | Protein: 1g | Cholesterol: 0mg | Sodium: 148.1mg

INGREDIENTS

- 1/3 cup red wine vinegar
- 1/3 cup olive oil
- 1 small onion, thinly sliced
- 1 teaspoon salt
- 2 tablespoons dried parsley
- 1 teaspoon ground dry mustard
- 1 tablespoon brown sugar
- 2 cloves garlic, peeled and crushed
- 1 pound small fresh button mushrooms

DIRECTIONS

1. In a medium saucepan, mix red wine vinegar, olive oil, onion, salt, parsley, dry mustard, brown sugar and garlic. Bring to a boil. Reduce heat. Stir in mushrooms. Simmer 10 to 12 minutes, stirring occasionally. Transfer to sterile containers and chill in the refrigerator until serving.

MUSHROOM AND SWISS CHICKEN

Servings: 4 | Prep: 25m | Cooks: 45m | Total: 1h10m

NUTRITION FACTS

Calories: 359.6 | Carbohydrates: 7.5g | Protein: 36.9g | Cholesterol: 94.5mg | Sodium: 499.9mg

INGREDIENTS

- 4 skinless, boneless chicken breasts
- 2 cloves crushed garlic
- 3 tablespoons olive oil
- 3 tablespoons red wine vinegar
- 1 tablespoon Cajun-style seasoning
- 1 cup chopped green onion
- 1 (8 ounce) package sliced fresh mushrooms
- 4 slices Swiss cheese

DIRECTIONS

1. Preheat oven to 350 degrees F (175 degrees C).
2. Combine oil and garlic in a 9x13 inch baking dish. Add chicken breasts and coat well with the oil and garlic. Sprinkle with the vinegar and Cajun seasoning.
3. Bake at 350 degrees F (175 degrees C) for 30 minutes.
4. Remove chicken from oven and cover with green onion and mushrooms; then add a few more sprinkles of oil and vinegar and return dish to oven for 15 to 20 minutes more. Remove from oven and immediately place 1 slice of cheese on top of each chicken breast; cheese will melt. Serve immediately.

ARTICHOKE STUFFED MUSHROOMS

Servings: 12 | Prep: 20m | Cooks: 25m | Total: 45m

NUTRITION FACTS

Calories: 155.9 | Carbohydrates: 6.3g | Protein: 6.3g | Cholesterol: 29.7mg | Sodium: 342.2mg

INGREDIENTS

- 1 tablespoon olive oil
- 1 onion, chopped
- 24 mushrooms, stems removed and chopped
- 1 pinch salt and ground black pepper to taste
- 1 (12 ounce) jar marinated artichoke hearts, drained and chopped
- 1 (8 ounce) package cream cheese, softened
- 2 tablespoons sour cream
- 1 cup shredded Italian cheese blend
- 2 tablespoons grated Parmesan cheese
- 1/2 teaspoon garlic salt, or to taste

DIRECTIONS

1. Preheat an oven to 350 degrees F (175 degrees C). Prepare a baking sheet with cooking spray.
2. Heat the olive oil in a skillet over medium heat; cook the onions and mushroom stems in the hot oil until the onion is translucent, about 5 minutes; season with salt and pepper. Transfer the mixture to a large bowl; add the artichoke hearts, cream cheese, sour cream, Italian cheese blend, and Parmesan cheese. Season with salt, pepper, and garlic salt. Stir the mixture until ingredients are evenly distributed. Stuff the mushroom caps with the mixture. Arrange the stuffed mushrooms on the prepared baking sheet.
3. Bake in the preheated oven until the filling begins to bubble, about 20 minutes.

BAKED HAVARTI CHICKEN

Servings: 4 | Prep: 20m | Cooks: 40m | Total: 1h30m | Additional: 30m

NUTRITION FACTS

Calories: 482.5 | Carbohydrates: 12.7g | Protein: 33.2g | Cholesterol: 109.8mg | Sodium: 2612.9mg

INGREDIENTS

- 4 boneless, skinless chicken breast halves
- 1 cup Italian dressing
- 1 tablespoon Greek seasoning, or to taste
- 1 tablespoon butter
- 1 tablespoon white cooking wine
- 1 tablespoon Worcestershire sauce
- 1/2 teaspoon garlic salt
- 1 (8 ounce) package sliced fresh mushrooms
- 1 pinch salt to taste
- 2 (4 ounce) cans whole green chili peppers, drained, and sliced lengthwise
- 4 ounces sliced Havarti cheese with dill

DIRECTIONS

1. Preheat oven to 400 degrees F (200 degrees C).
2. Marinate chicken in Italian dressing and Greek seasoning in a bowl, at least 30 minutes.
3. Place chicken in a 9x13-inch baking dish. Sprinkle top with additional Greek seasoning.
4. Bake in preheated oven until no longer pink in center and juices run clear, about 25 minutes. An instant-read thermometer inserted into the center should read at least 165 degrees F (74 degrees C).
5. Melt butter in a skillet over medium-high heat until bubbling. Pour in wine, Worcestershire sauce, and garlic salt; bring to a boil. Stir in mushrooms; reduce to a simmer, cover, and cook until mushrooms are tender, about 3 to 5 minutes. Seasoning mixture with salt.

6. Arrange green chili peppers lengthwise and Havarti cheese on top of chicken. Return to the oven and bake until cheese has melted, about 5 minutes. Top chicken with mushrooms and pan juices.

JAPANESE BEEF STIR-FRY

Servings: 8 | Prep: 30m | Cooks: 15m | Total: 45m

NUTRITION FACTS

Calories: 289.8 | Carbohydrates: 26.4g | Protein: 26.4g | Cholesterol: 38.9mg | Sodium: 1270.7mg

INGREDIENTS

- 2 pounds boneless beef sirloin or beef top round steaks (3/4" thick)
- 3 tablespoons cornstarch
- 1 (10.5 ounce) can Campbell's® Condensed Beef Broth
- 1/2 cup soy sauce
- 2 tablespoons sugar
- 2 tablespoons vegetable oil
- 4 cups sliced shiitake mushrooms
- 1 head Chinese cabbage (bok choy), thinly sliced
- 2 medium red peppers, cut into 2"-long strips
- 3 stalks celery, sliced
- 2 medium green onions, cut into 2" pieces
- 2 cups Hot cooked regular long-grain white rice

DIRECTIONS

1. Slice beef into very thin strips.
2. Mix cornstarch, broth, soy and sugar until smooth. Set aside.
3. Heat 1 tablespoon oil in saucepot or wok over high heat. Add beef in 2 batches and stir-fry until browned. Set beef aside.
4. Add 1 tablespoon oil. Add the mushrooms, cabbage, peppers, celery and green onions in 2 batches and stir-fry over medium heat until tender-crisp. Set vegetables aside.
5. Stir cornstarch mixture and add. Cook until mixture boils and thickens, stirring constantly. Return beef and vegetables to saucepot and heat through. Serve over rice.

TURKEY A LA KING

Servings: 4 | Prep: 10m | Cooks: 15m | Total: 25m

NUTRITION FACTS

Calories: 232.8 | Carbohydrates: 4.5g | Protein: 12.2g | Cholesterol: 82.6mg | Sodium: 91.5mg

INGREDIENTS

- 2 tablespoons butter
- 3 fresh mushrooms, sliced
- 1 tablespoon all-purpose flour
- 1 cup chicken broth
- 1/2 cup heavy cream
- 1 cup chopped cooked turkey
- 1/3 cup frozen peas, thawed
- salt and pepper to taste

DIRECTIONS

1. In a large skillet over medium low heat, cook butter until golden brown. Saute mushrooms until tender. Stir in flour until smooth. Slowly whisk in chicken broth, and cook until slightly thickened. Stir in cream, turkey and peas. Reduce heat to low, and cook until thickened. Season with salt and pepper.

CHICKEN CACCIATORE

Servings: 6 | Prep: 20m | Cooks: 1h30m | Total: 1h50m

NUTRITION FACTS

Calories: 512.8 | Carbohydrates: 11.1g | Protein: 50.2g | Cholesterol: 149.4mg | Sodium: 400.9mg

INGREDIENTS

- 2 tablespoons olive oil
- 1 whole roasting chicken, cut in quarters
- 1 large onion, sliced
- 8 ounces fresh mushrooms, quartered
- 1 pinch salt
- 1 pinch ground black pepper
- 1 teaspoon dried oregano
- 1/2 teaspoon red pepper flakes, or to taste
- 1 cup tomato sauce
- 1/2 cup water
- 1 pinch salt and ground black pepper to taste
- 2 red bell peppers, sliced

- 4 cloves garlic, sliced
- 3 sprigs rosemary
- 2 green bell peppers, sliced

DIRECTIONS

1. Preheat the oven to 350 degrees F (175 degrees C).
2. Heat olive oil in a large Dutch oven over medium-high heat; add chicken and cook until browned on the outside. Remove to a bowl to capture the juices.
3. Stir in onions and mushrooms; cook for 5-6 minutes until soft. Add a big pinch of salt and pepper. Stir in garlic, rosemary, red pepper flakes, oregano, tomato sauce, and water.
4. Place chicken pieces and any juices that have accumulated in the bowl on top of the cooked vegetables. Add more salt and pepper. Place pepper slices on top of the chicken.
5. Cover and cook in the preheated oven for 1 hour 15 minutes.

BOB'S MEXICAN STUFFED CHICKEN
Servings: 4 | Prep: 30m | Cooks: 40m | Total: 1h10m

NUTRITION FACTS

Calories: 367.7 | Carbohydrates: 24.6g | Protein: 35.2g | Cholesterol: 103.4mg | Sodium: 1105.3mg

INGREDIENTS

- 2 cups crushed corn flakes
- 1 tablespoon chili powder
- 1 (1.27 ounce) packet dry fajita seasoning
- 1/4cup chopped red bell pepper
- 1/4cup chopped yellow bell pepper
- 1/4cup chopped orange bell pepper
- 1/3 cup chopped fresh mushrooms
- 1/2 medium red onion, diced
- 4 skinless, boneless chicken breast halves - pounded thin
- 1 cup shredded Cheddar cheese, divided
- 1/4 cup salsa
- 1 box toothpicks

DIRECTIONS

1. Preheat oven to 350 degrees F (175 degrees C). Lightly grease a baking dish.
2. In a shallow bowl, mix the corn flakes, chili powder, and fajita seasoning. In a separate bowl, mix the red bell pepper, yellow bell pepper, orange bell pepper, mushrooms, and onion.

3. Dredge the chicken in the corn flakes mixture to evenly coat. Sprinkle one side of each breast with 2 tablespoons Cheddar cheese, and layer with 1/4 the vegetable mixture. Top with equal amounts salsa. Carefully roll the breast halves over the filling. Seal seams with toothpicks, then dredge again in the corn flakes mixture.

4. Arrange the rolled chicken breasts in the prepared baking dish. Bake 30 minutes in the preheated oven. Top with remaining cheese, and continue baking 10 minutes, or until chicken juices run clear and cheese is melted.

PASTA SHELLS WITH PORTOBELLO MUSHROOMS AND ASPARAGUS IN BOURSIN SAUCE

Servings: 6 | Prep: 15m | Cooks: 25m | Total: 40m

NUTRITION FACTS

Calories: 400 | Carbohydrates: 51.6g | Protein: 14.1g | Cholesterol: 35.1mg | Sodium: 388.4mg

INGREDIENTS

- 1 tablespoon butter
- 1 tablespoon olive oil
- 1 pound portobello mushrooms, stems removed
- 1/2 teaspoon salt
- 1 1/4 cups low-sodium chicken broth
- 1 (5.2 ounce) package pepper Boursin cheese
- 3/4 pound uncooked pasta shells
- 1 pound fresh asparagus, trimmed

DIRECTIONS

1. In a large skillet over medium heat, melt the butter and heat the olive oil. Cut the mushroom caps in half, and slice 1/4 inch thick. Cook mushrooms in the skillet 8 minutes, or until tender and lightly browned. Season with salt. Stir in the chicken broth and Boursin cheese. Reduce heat and simmer, stirring constantly, until well blended.

2. Bring a large pot of lightly salted water to a boil. Add shell pasta and cook for 5 minutes. Place the asparagus into the pot, and continue cooking 5 minutes, until the pasta is al dente and the asparagus is tender; drain. Toss with the mushroom sauce to serve.

SHAKSHUKA

Servings: 6 | Prep: 15m | Cooks: 30m | Total: 45m

NUTRITION FACTS

Calories: 185.2 | Carbohydrates: 14.9g | Protein: 9.9g | Cholesterol: 188.8mg | Sodium: 669.8mg

INGREDIENTS

- 2 tablespoons olive oil
- 1 large onion, diced
- 1/2 cup sliced fresh mushrooms
- 1 teaspoon salt, or more to taste
- 1 cup diced red bell pepper
- 1 jalapeno pepper, seeded and sliced
- 1 teaspoon cumin
- 1/2 teaspoon paprika
- 1/2 teaspoon ground turmeric
- 1/2 teaspoon freshly ground black pepper, plus more to taste
- 1/4 teaspoon cayenne pepper
- 1 (28 ounce) can crushed San Marzano tomatoes, or other high-quality plum tomatoes
- 1/2 cup water, or more as needed
- 6 large eggs
- 2 tablespoons crumbled feta cheese
- 2 tablespoons chopped fresh parsley

DIRECTIONS

1. Heat olive oil in a large, heavy skillet over medium-high heat. Add onions and mushrooms. Sprinkle with salt. Cook and stir until mushrooms release all of their liquid and start to brown, about 10 minutes. Stir in bell peppers and jalapeno pepper. Cook and stir until peppers begin to soften up, about 5 minutes. Season with cumin, paprika, turmeric, black pepper, and cayenne. Stir and cook to "wake up" the flavors, about 1 minute. Pour in crushed tomatoes and water. Adjust heat to medium and simmer uncovered until veggies are softened and sweet, stirring occasionally, 15 to 20 minutes. Add more water if sauce becomes too thick.
2. Make a depression in the sauce for each egg with a large spoon. Crack egg into a small ramekin and slide gently into each indentation; repeat with the rest of the eggs. Season with salt and pepper. Cover and cook until eggs are to your desired doneness
3. Top with feta cheese and parsley.

WINTER VEGETABLE HASH

Servings: 6 | Prep: 15m | Cooks: 35m | Total: 50m

NUTRITION FACTS

Calories: 223 | Carbohydrates: 28.9g | Fat: 10.9g | Protein: 4.1g | Cholesterol: 10mg | Sodium: 76mg

INGREDIENTS

- 3 tablespoons olive oil
- 2 tablespoons butter
- 1 pound Yukon Gold potatoes, diced
- 1/2 pound fresh shiitake mushrooms, diced
- 1 red bell pepper, diced
- 1 small acorn squash, diced
- 1 shallot, finely chopped
- 2 teaspoons garlic powder
- 1 pinch salt
- 1 pinch ground black pepper
- 1 cup chopped kale
- 4 sprigs fresh sage

DIRECTIONS

1. Place oil and butter in a large skillet over medium heat. Melt butter and mix in potatoes, mushrooms, pepper, squash, and shallot. Season with garlic powder, salt, and pepper. Cook 25 minutes, stirring occasionally, until potatoes are tender.
2. Mix kale and sage into skillet. Continue cooking 5 minutes, until kale is wilted. Serve and enjoy.

SPINACH AND MUSHROOM QUESADILLAS

Servings: 16 | Prep: 10m | Cooks: 25m | Total: 35m

NUTRITION FACTS

Calories: 154.1 | Carbohydrates: 10.9g | Protein: 6.7g | Cholesterol: 21.9mg | Sodium: 246.5mg

INGREDIENTS

- 1 (10 ounce) package chopped spinach
- 2 cups shredded Cheddar cheese
- 2 tablespoons butter
- 2 cloves garlic, sliced
- 2 portobello mushroom caps, sliced
- 4 (10 inch) flour tortillas
- 1 tablespoon vegetable oil

DIRECTIONS

1. Prepare spinach according to package directions. Drain and pat dry.
2. Preheat oven to 350 degrees F (175 degrees C). Sprinkle 1/2 cup cheese on one side of each tortilla. Place tortillas cheese side up on baking sheets, and bake 5 minutes, or until cheese is melted.
3. Melt the butter in a skillet over medium heat. Stir in garlic and mushrooms, and cook about 5 minutes. Mix in spinach, and continue cooking 5 minutes. Place an equal amount of the mixture on the cheese side of each tortilla. Fold tortillas in half over the filling.
4. Heat oil in a separate skillet over medium heat. Place quesadillas in the skillet one at a time, and cook 3 minutes on each side, until golden brown. Cut each quesadilla into 4 wedges to serve.

SPINACH MUSHROOM QUICHE

Servings: 6 | Prep: 25m | Cooks: 30m | Total: 55m

NUTRITION FACTS

Calories: 342.7 | Carbohydrates: 22.8g | Protein: 15g | Cholesterol: 177.1mg | Sodium: 704.8mg

INGREDIENTS

- 2 tablespoons butter
- 2 cups fresh sliced mushrooms
- 2 cups torn spinach leaves
- 6 green onions, chopped
- 1 (8 ounce) package refrigerated crescent rolls
- 1 (1 ounce) package herb and lemon soup mix
- 1/2 cup half-and-half
- 4 eggs, beaten
- 1 cup shredded Monterey Jack cheese

DIRECTIONS

1. Preheat oven to 375 degrees F (190 degrees C).
2. Melt margarine in a skillet over medium heat and cook mushrooms, spinach and onions for 5 minutes or until tender, stir continuously. Remove the skillet from heat.
3. In a 9 inch round pan or pie plate coated with non-stick cooking spray arrange crescent roll triangles in a circle, with narrow tips hung over the rim of the pie plate about 2 inches. Press dough onto the bottom and side of the pie plate to fill in any gaps.
4. In a medium bowl stir together the soup mix, half and half cream and eggs. Stir the cheese and cooked vegetables into the egg mixture until blended. Pour into the prepared crust. Fold the points of dough that are hanging over the edge back in over the filling.
5. Bake the quiche for 30 minutes in the preheated oven, or until a knife inserted into the center comes out clean.

CHICKEN GRUYERE WITH SAUTEED MUSHROOMS

Servings: 4 | Prep: 15m | Cooks: 30m | Total: 45m

NUTRITION FACTS

Calories: 557 | Carbohydrates: 13.5g | Protein: 46.2g | Cholesterol: 160mg | Sodium: 630.4mg

INGREDIENTS

- 1/4 cup all-purpose flour
- 1/2 teaspoon salt
- 1/4teaspoon pepper
- 1 teaspoon chopped fresh parsley
- 1/2 teaspoon dried dill weed
- 1/4cup butter, divided
- 4 boneless, skinless chicken breast halves
- 1 pound fresh mushrooms
- 1 onion, sliced into rings
- 1/2 cup white wine
- 8 ounces Gruyere cheese, shredded

DIRECTIONS

1. Preheat the oven to 350 degrees F (175 degrees C). In a shallow dish, stir together the flour, salt, pepper, parsley, and dill. Rinse chicken breasts, and pat dry. Dredge chicken in the flour mixture.
2. In a large skillet, heat 2 tablespoons of the butter over medium-high heat. Place chicken into the hot buttered skillet, and fry until brown on both sides. Transfer chicken breasts to a 1 quart glass baking dish. Add remaining butter to skillet, and fry the mushrooms and onion until wilted and lightly browned. Stir in the white wine, and reduce heat to medium. Simmer for 3 minutes to blend flavors. Pour the mushroom mixture over the chicken in the dish.
3. Cover dish, and bake for 20 minutes in the preheated oven. After 20 minutes, remove cover, and sprinkle with shredded cheese. Continue baking for 10 more minutes, or until cheese is lightly browned and bubbly.

SOUTHERN FRIED CABBAGE WITH BACON, MUSHROOMS, AND ONIONS

Servings: 10 | Prep: 15m | Cooks: 30m | Total: 45m

NUTRITION FACTS

Calories: 122.7 | Carbohydrates: 9.6g | Protein: 8g | Cholesterol: 16.4mg | Sodium: 368.4mg

INGREDIENTS

- 1 pound bacon
- 1 large head cabbage, chopped
- 1 large onion, chopped
- 1 (8 ounce) package sliced fresh mushrooms
- 1 pinch salt and ground black pepper to taste

DIRECTIONS

1. Place bacon in a large skillet and cook over medium-high heat, turning occasionally, until evenly browned, about 10 minutes. Drain the bacon slices on paper towels; crumble when cooled. Drain all but 3 tablespoons of bacon drippings from skillet.
2. Cook and stir cabbage, onion, and mushrooms in the remaining bacon drippings until tender and lightly browned, about 20 minutes. Fold bacon into cabbage mixture. Season with salt and black pepper.

NORTHERN ITALIAN BEEF STEW

Servings: 8 | Prep: 30m | Cooks: 4h20m | Total: 4h50m

NUTRITION FACTS

Calories: 475.7 | Carbohydrates: 34.4g | Protein: 49.9g | Cholesterol: 102mg | Sodium: 500.5mg

INGREDIENTS

- 2 tablespoons olive oil
- 2 pounds lean top round, trimmed and cut into 1-inch cubes
- 2 large sweet onions, diced
- 2 cups large chunks of celery
- 4 large carrots, peeled and cut into large rounds
- 1 pound crimini mushrooms, sliced
- 2 tablespoons minced garlic
- 2 cups dry red wine
- 4 large tomatoes, chopped
- 1 1/2 pounds red potatoes (such as Red Bliss), cut into 1-inch chunks
- 1 tablespoon dried basil
- 1 teaspoon dried thyme
- 1 teaspoon dried marjoram
- 1/2 teaspoon dried sage
- 1 quart beef stock
- 2 cups tomato sauce

DIRECTIONS

1. Heat olive oil in a large skillet over medium-high heat. Cook beef in batches in hot oil until browned completely, about 5 minutes per batch. Remove browned beef cubes to a plate lined with paper towels, keeping skillet over heat and retaining the beef drippings.
2. Cook and stir onion, celery, and carrots in the retained beef drippings until just softened, 2 to 3 minutes. Stir mushrooms and garlic into the onion mixture.
3. Pour red wine into the pan; bring to a boil while scraping the browned bits of food off the bottom of the pan with a wooden spoon. Continue cooking the mixture until the wine evaporates, 7 to 10 minutes. Stir tomatoes into the mixture.
4. Return beef to skillet with potatoes, basil, thyme, marjoram, and sage. Pour beef stock and tomato sauce over the mixture. Bring the liquid to a simmer.
5. Reduce heat to low and simmer until the beef is very tender and the sauce is thick, 4 to 6 hours.

CREAMY MUSHROOM MEATLOAF

Servings: 8 | Prep: 15m | Cooks: 2h | Total: 2h15m

NUTRITION FACTS

Calories: 324 | Carbohydrates: 13.6g | Fat: 16.5g | Protein: 27.9g | Cholesterol: 139mg | Sodium: 501mg

INGREDIENTS

- 1/4 cup butter
- 2 cups shiitake mushrooms, sliced
- 1 pinch salt
- 1 sprig fresh rosemary, chopped
- 3 tablespoons all-purpose flour
- 2 1/2 cups beef broth
- salt and pepper to taste
- 1/2 cup heavy cream
- 1 (2 1/2 pound) uncooked prepared beef, veal and pork meatloaf

DIRECTIONS

1. Preheat the oven to 325 degrees F (165 degrees C).
2. Melt butter in an oven-safe skillet over medium-high heat. Stir in mushrooms and a pinch of salt; cook and stir until mushrooms begin to brown, about 5 minutes.
3. Stir in fresh rosemary. Add flour and stir to coat the mushrooms; cook and stir for about 3 minutes.
4. Whisk in beef broth, 1/2 cup at a time, whisking constantly to prevent lumps.
5. Turn heat to high and bring the sauce to a simmer. Simmer a few minutes until sauce starts to thicken. Season with salt and pepper to taste.
6. Remove from heat and stir in heavy cream.

7. Slide prepared meatloaf into the sauce. Spoon sauce over the top of the meatloaf.

8. Bake in the preheated oven until no longer pink in the center, about 1 1/2 hours. An instant-read thermometer inserted into the center should read at least 160 degrees F (70 degrees C).

9. Remove pan from the oven and gently remove meatloaf to a serving platter.

10. Skim off any extra fat from the surface of the sauce.

11. Bring the sauce to a boil over medium-high heat to reduce until thick, about 5 minutes.

ZITI WITH ITALIAN SAUSAGE

Servings: 8 | Prep: 15m | Cooks: 1h15m | Total: 1h30m

NUTRITION FACTS

Calories: 464.6 | Carbohydrates: 52.3g | Protein: 24.6g | Cholesterol: 42.7mg | Sodium: 1620mg

INGREDIENTS

- 1 pound Italian sausage, casings removed
- 1/2 cup diced celery
- 1/2 cup diced onion
- 1 (14.5 ounce) can peeled and diced tomatoes
- 1 (15 ounce) can tomato sauce
- 1/4 teaspoon garlic powder
- 1 1/2 teaspoons salt
- 1 teaspoon dried oregano
- 1 pound dry ziti pasta
- 2 (4.5 ounce) cans sliced mushrooms, drained
- 8 ounces shredded mozzarella cheese
- 1/4 cup grated Parmesan cheese

DIRECTIONS

1. In a skillet over medium heat, cook sausage with celery and onion until sausage is evenly browned, about 5 to 10 minutes. Drain excess grease, and set aside.

2. In another skillet over medium-low heat, combine tomatoes, tomato sauce, garlic powder, salt, and oregano. Simmer while preparing pasta.

3. Bring a large pot of lightly salted water to a boil. Cook pasta for 8 to 10 minutes, or until al dente; drain.

4. Preheat oven to 350 degrees F (175 degrees C). In a 3 quart baking dish, layer ziti, mushrooms, sausage, mozzarella cheese, and sauce. Repeat layers, and top with grated Parmesan.

5. Bake for 45 minutes in the preheated oven, or until browned and bubbly.

PORK BUTT ROAST WITH VEGETABLES

Servings: 8 | Prep: 20m | Cooks: 4h | Total: 4h20m

NUTRITION FACTS

Calories: 541.1 | Carbohydrates: 46g | Protein: 43.5g | Cholesterol: 123.5mg | Sodium: 277.2mg

INGREDIENTS

- salt and pepper to taste
- garlic powder to taste
- 6 pounds pork butt roast
- 2 onion, sliced
- 20 eaches new potatoes, raw
- 16 carrots, peeled
- 2 cups mushrooms, halved

DIRECTIONS

1. Preheat oven to 350 degrees F (175 degrees C).
2. Heat a large frying pan over medium high heat. Sprinkle pork on all sides with salt, pepper and garlic powder; rub into meat. Sear the meat on all sides until lightly brown. Transfer to a roasting pan.
3. Place onion slices over meat and in the roasting pan. Fill the pan 2/3 full of water. Cover and place in preheated oven for 3 hours. Add the potatoes and carrots; cover and cook 45 minutes. Add the mushrooms and cook another 15 minutes. Remove and let stand at least 10 minutes before serving.

CREAM OF MUSHROOM SOUP

Servings: 4 | Prep: 15m | Cooks: 15m | Total: 30m

NUTRITION FACTS

Calories: 296.6 | Carbohydrates: 15.9g | Protein: 7.1g | Cholesterol: 70.1mg | Sodium: 574.3mg

INGREDIENTS

- 1 pound fresh mushrooms
- 1/4 cup salted butter
- 4 green onions, thinly sliced
- 3 cloves garlic, chopped
- 4 cups vegetable broth
- 1 cup light cream
- salt and pepper to taste
- 1 sprig fresh thyme leaves

- 1 teaspoon chopped fresh thyme
- 2 tablespoons all-purpose flour
- 1 tablespoon chopped fresh chives

DIRECTIONS

1. Thinly slice the mushroom caps, discarding the stalks.
2. Melt the butter in a heavy-based pan and cook the spring onion, garlic and lemon thyme, stirring, for 1 minute, or until the garlic is golden. Add the mushroom and salt and white pepper. Cook for 3 to 4 minutes, or until the mushroom just softens. Add flour and cook, stirring for 1 minute.
3. Remove from the heat and add the stock, stirring continuously. Return to the heat and bring to the boil, stirring. Reduce the heat and simmer gently for 2 minutes, stirring occasionally.
4. Whisk the cream into the soup, then reheat gently, stirring. Do not allow the soup to boil. Season to taste with salt and pepper, and garnish with the chopped chives and thyme.

VEGGIE PITA PIZZA

Servings: 1 | Prep: 5m | Cooks: 15m | Total: 20m

NUTRITION FACTS

Calories: 405.2 | Carbohydrates: 39.9g | Protein: 19.7g | Cholesterol: 44.2mg | Sodium: 1155.9mg

INGREDIENTS

- 1 pita bread round
- 1 teaspoon olive oil
- 3 tablespoons pizza sauce
- 1/2 cup shredded mozzarella cheese
- 1/4 cup sliced crimini mushrooms
- 1/8 teaspoon garlic salt

DIRECTIONS

1. Preheat grill for medium-high heat.
2. Spread one side of the pita with olive oil and pizza sauce. Top with cheese and mushrooms, and season with garlic salt.
3. Lightly oil grill grate. Place pita pizza on grill, cover, and cook until cheese completely melts, about 5 minutes.

BRUSSELS SPROUTS IN A SHERRY BACON CREAM SAUCE

Servings: 4 | Prep: 20m | Cooks: 35m | Total: 1h55m | Additional: 1h

NUTRITION FACTS

Calories: 370.6 | Carbohydrates: 16.9g | Protein: 9g | Cholesterol: 59.8mg | Sodium: 2190.1mg

INGREDIENTS

- 1 tablespoon salt
- 1 pound Brussels sprouts, trimmed and halved lengthwise
- 2 tablespoons olive oil
- 1 pinch sea salt and freshly ground black pepper to taste
- 4 slices bacon, chopped
- 1 shallot, chopped
- 7 cremini mushrooms, chopped, or more to taste
- 1 clove garlic, minced
- 1/4 cup cream sherry
- 1/2 cup heavy cream

DIRECTIONS

1. Dissolve 1 tablespoon of salt in enough water to cover the Brussels sprouts in a bowl, and soak the sprouts in the salty water for 1 hour. Drain off the water, and toss the sprouts in olive oil, sea salt, and black pepper to coat thoroughly.
2. Preheat oven to 475 degrees F (245 degrees C).
3. Place the bacon in a large, deep skillet, and cook over medium-high heat, stirring occasionally, until just beginning to brown at the edges, 5 to 8 minutes. Reduce heat to medium; stir in the shallot and mushrooms, then cook until the shallots turn translucent, about 5 more minutes. Sprinkle in the garlic, and cook 1 minute, then stir in the sherry and cream until well combined. Bring the mixture to a boil, and stir until reduced by half. The thickened sauce should coat the back of a spoon.
4. While the sauce is cooking, lay the Brussels sprouts, cut sides down, onto a baking sheet, and bake in the preheated oven until the sprouts are browned, about 15 minutes. Transfer the browned sprouts to the sauce, toss to coat, and season to taste with salt and black pepper.

MUSHROOM SOUP WITHOUT CREAM

Servings: 8 | Prep: 15m | Cooks: 45m | Total: 1h

NUTRITION FACTS

Calories: 80.5 | Carbohydrates: 9.6g | Protein: 4.6g | Cholesterol: 8.2mg | Sodium: 560.9mg

INGREDIENTS

- 2 tablespoons butter
- 1 cup peeled and sliced carrots
- 1 cup sliced onions
- 1 cup sliced leeks
- 1/2 cup sliced celery
- 1 teaspoon fresh thyme leaves
- 2 pounds sliced fresh brown or white mushrooms
- 6 cups chicken stock
- salt and pepper to taste
- 1/2 cup chopped green onion

DIRECTIONS

1. Melt the butter in a stock pot over medium heat. Add carrots, onions, leeks, and celery. Cook and stir until tender, but not browned, about 10 minutes. Stir in thyme and mushrooms, and continue cooking until mushrooms are soft, about 5 minutes.
2. Pour chicken stock into the pot, and season with salt and pepper. Cover, and simmer over low heat for 30 minutes. Ladle into bowls, and serve with green onions sprinkled on the top.

HONEY CURRIED ROASTED CHICKEN AND VEGETABLES

Servings: 6 | Prep: 15m | Cooks: 1h30m | Total: 1h45m

NUTRITION FACTS

Calories: 625.2 | Carbohydrates: 70.7g | Protein: 35.4g | Cholesterol: 112.3mg | Sodium: 716.3mg

INGREDIENTS

- 1 (3 pound) whole chicken
- 4 medium red potatoes, peeled and quartered
- 6 carrots, cut into 1/2 inch pieces
- 2/3 cup honey
- 1/3 cup Dijon mustard
- 3 tablespoons butter
- 2 1/2 teaspoons curry powder
- 1/2 teaspoon salt
- 1/4 teaspoon red pepper flakes
- 1/4 teaspoon ground ginger
- 1/4 teaspoon finely chopped garlic
- 12 whole fresh mushrooms

- 2 tablespoons finely chopped onion
- 2 apples, cored and quartered

DIRECTIONS

1. Preheat oven to 350 degrees F (175 degrees C).
2. Place the chicken breast side down on a rack in a roasting pan, and roast 1 hour in the preheated oven.
3. Place the potatoes and carrots in a pot with enough water to cover, and bring to a boil. Cook 20 minutes, or until tender.
4. In a saucepan, mix the honey, mustard, butter, onion, curry powder, salt, cayenne pepper, ginger, and garlic. Bring to a boil, stirring constantly. Remove from heat, and set aside.
5. Drain the drippings from the roasting pan. Arrange the potatoes, carrots, mushrooms, and apples around the chicken. Drizzle the chicken and vegetables with the honey mixture. Continue roasting 20 minutes, or until the glaze has browned. The chicken meat should reach an internal temperature of 180 degrees F (85 degrees C).

ROLLED FLANK STEAK

Servings: 6 | Prep: 45m | Cooks: 1h | Total: 5h45m | Additional: 4h

NUTRITION FACTS

Calories: 472.5 | Carbohydrates: 3g | Protein: 31.4g | Cholesterol: 66.7mg | Sodium: 1421.5mg

INGREDIENTS

- 1 (2 pound) beef flank steak
- 1/4 cup soy sauce
- 1/2 cup olive oil
- 2 teaspoons steak seasoning
- 8 ounces thinly sliced provolone cheese
- 4 slices thick cut bacon
- 1/2 cup fresh spinach leaves
- 1/2 cup sliced crimini mushrooms
- 1/2 red bell pepper, seeded and cut into strips

DIRECTIONS

1. Place the flank steak on a cutting board with the short end closest to you. Starting from one of the long sides, cut through the meat horizontally to within 1/2 inch of the opposite edge. (You can also ask your butcher to butterfly the flank steak for you instead of cutting it yourself.)
2. Mix the soy sauce, olive oil, and steak seasoning together in a gallon-sized resealable plastic bag. Marinate flank steak in the refrigerator 4 hours to overnight.

3. Preheat oven to 350 degrees F (175 degrees C). Grease a glass baking dish.

4. Lay out the flank steak flat in front of you with the grain of the meat running from left to right. Layer the provolone across the steak, leaving a 1-inch border. Arrange the bacon, spinach, red pepper, and mushrooms across the cheese covered steak in stripes running in the same direction as the grain of the meat. Roll the flank steak up and away from you, so that when the roll is cut into the pinwheel shape, each of the filling ingredients can be seen. Roll firmly, but be careful not to squeeze the fillings out the ends. Once rolled, tie every 2 inches with kitchen twine.

5. Place in prepared baking dish, and bake in preheated oven for one hour, or until the internal temperature reaches 145 degrees F (65 degrees C). Remove from the oven and let rest for 5 to 10 minutes before cutting into 1 inch slices. Be sure to remove the twine before serving.

JALAPENO POPPER MUSHROOMS

Servings: 4 | Prep: 20m | Cooks: 35m | Total: 55m

NUTRITION FACTS

Calories: 150.8 | Carbohydrates: 2.5g | Protein: 6.1g | Cholesterol: 34.9mg | Sodium: 287.7mg

INGREDIENTS

- 2 slices bacon
- 1 serving cooking spray
- 1 1/2 teaspoons olive oil
- 8 mushrooms, stems removed and chopped and caps reserved
- 1 clove garlic, minced
- 1 jalapeno pepper, ribs and seeds removed, finely chopped
- 1 (3 ounce) package cream cheese, softened
- 3 tablespoons shredded Cheddar cheese
- 1 pinch sea salt to taste
- 1 pinch ground black pepper to taste

DIRECTIONS

1. Place the bacon in a large, deep skillet, and cook over medium-high heat, turning occasionally, until evenly browned, about 10 minutes. Drain the bacon slices on a paper towel-lined plate. Crumble the bacon slices and set aside.

2. Preheat an oven to 350 degrees F (175 degrees C). Spray a baking dish with cooking spray.

3. Heat the olive oil in a skillet over medium heat. Stir in the chopped mushroom stems, garlic, and jalapeno; cook and stir until the mushrooms release moisture and soften, about 10 minutes. Transfer the mushroom mixture to a bowl, and stir in the cream cheese, cheddar cheese, and bacon. Season with salt and pepper. Spoon the cheese mixture generously into the reserved mushroom caps, and arrange the stuffed caps on the prepared baking dish.

4. Bake in the preheated oven until cheese begins to brown, 15 to 20 minutes.

BAKED MUSHROOM RICE

Servings: 6 | Prep: 15m | Cooks: 40m | Total: 55m

NUTRITION FACTS

Calories: 363.5 | Carbohydrates: 57.9g | Protein: 6.3g | Cholesterol: 20.3mg | Sodium: 461.9mg

INGREDIENTS

- 2 cups uncooked white rice
- 1 (10.75 ounce) can condensed cream of mushroom soup
- 1 cup vegetable broth
- 1/2 cup chopped onion
- 1/4 cup fresh chopped mushrooms
- 1 teaspoon dried parsley
- 1 teaspoon dried oregano
- 1/4 cup butter, melted
- salt and pepper to taste

DIRECTIONS

1. Preheat oven to 400 degrees F (200 degrees C).
2. In a large bowl, stir together the white rice, cream of mushroom soup, and vegetable broth. Blend in the onion, mushrooms, parsley, oregano, melted butter, salt, and pepper. Transfer to a 2 quart baking dish, and cover with a lid or aluminum foil.
3. Bake for 35 to 40 minutes in the preheated oven. If the rice is looking dry before it is tender, then pour in a little water and continue cooking until rice is tender.

MUSHROOM MEATLOAF

Servings: 4 | Prep: 15m | Cooks: 1h45m | Total: 2h

NUTRITION FACTS

Calories: 765.3 | Carbohydrates: 26.2g | Protein: 48.5g | Cholesterol: 263.3mg | Sodium: 1549.9mg

INGREDIENTS

- 2 pounds lean ground beef
- 1/2 pound fresh mushrooms, all minced
- 1/2 cup ketchup
- 2 eggs, beaten

except for 6

- 3/4 cup fresh bread crumbs
- 1/2 cup minced onion
- 1 1/2 teaspoons salt
- 1/2 teaspoon ground black pepper

DIRECTIONS

1. Preheat oven to 350 degrees F (175 degrees C).
2. In a large mixing bowl, combine ground meat, minced mushrooms, bread crumbs, onion, ketchup, eggs, and salt and pepper. Mix well. Spread 1/2 of the mixture into the bottom of a loaf pan. Arrange 6 whole mushrooms stem down into meat. Top with rest of meat, patting to combine both halves.
3. Bake for 1 hour and 45 minutes, or until done. Internal temperature should measure 160 degrees F (70 degrees C) when done.